DONALD W. TREADGOLD STUDIES
ON
RUSSIA, EAST EUROPE, AND CENTRAL ASIA

The Editor of Treadgold Studies is Glennys Young,
Associate Professor of History and International Studies,
University of Washington.

From 1994 to 2001, the Editor of Treadgold Papers
was Professor Sabrina Ramet.

Books in the Treadgold Studies series honor the memory
and distinguished contributions of Donald W. Treadgold,
who taught Russian history at the
University of Washington from 1949 to 1993.

*Perils of Pankratova Some: Stories from the Annals
of Soviet Historiography* (2005)
Reginald E. Zelnik

*Plays of Expectations: Intertextual Relations in
Russian Twentieth-Century Drama* (2006)
Andrew Baruch Wachtel

PLAYS OF EXPECTATIONS
Intertextual Relations in Russian Twentieth-Century Drama

Andrew Baruch Wachtel

Published by the Herbert J. Ellison Center for Russian,
East European, and Central Asian Studies, University of Washington

Distributed by the University of Washington Press
Seattle and London

Printed in the United States of America
12 11 10 09 08 07 06   5 4 3 2 1

Russian, East European, and Central Asian Studies Center (REECAS)
Henry M. Jackson School of International Studies, University of Washington
www.depts.washington.edu/reecas
For more information about the Treadgold Series and previously published Treadgold Papers, visit www.jsis.washington/edu/ellison/outreach_treadgold.shtml

University of Washington Press
P.O. Box 50096, Seattle, WA 98145-5096
www.washington.edu/uwpress

Library of Congress Cataloging-in-Publication Data
Wachtel, Andrew.
Plays of expectations : intertextual relations in Russian twentieth-century drama / Andrew Baruch Wachtel.
p. cm. – (Donald W. Treadgold studies on Russia, East Europe, and Central Asia)
Includes bibliographical references.
ISBN-13: 978-0-295-98647-0; ISBN-10: 0-295-98647-6 (pbk. : alk. paper)
1. Russian drama—20th century—History and criticism. 2. Intertextuality.
3. Theater—Russia (Federation)—History—20th century. 4. Expectation (Psychology) in literature. I. Title.
PG3086.W29   2006
891.72'4092–dc22   2006020409

CONTENTS

ACKNOWLEDGMENTS

MY INITIAL INTEREST in the study of Russian theater and drama was sparked many years ago by a series of inspired lectures on this topic by Jurij Striedter. Jurij always said that he wanted to write a book with a title similar to the one I have chosen for this volume, so I would like to thank him both for starting me down this path and for helping to name it. Further interest in this topic was piqued by lectures and conversations with Simon Karlinsky, whose inspiration I wish to acknowledge as well.

A number of pieces in this volume have been published previously. Chapter 1 is a slightly modified version of an article that appeared originally in PMLA as "Resurrection à la Russe: Tolstoy's play *The Living Corpse* in its Cultural Context" (March 1992). Chapter 4 has been adapted from my contribution to the book *Petrushka: Sources and Contexts* (Evanston, IL: Northwestern University Press). Chapter 5 appeared in the volume *Epic Revisionism: Tsarist-Era Heroes in Stalinist Mass Culture and Propaganda*, edited by David Brandenberger and Kevin Platt (Madison: University of Wisconsin Press, 2006). Finally, chapter 7 is reprinted with permission from *Word, Music, History: A Festschrift for Caryl Emerson*, edited by Lazar Fleishman, Gabriella Safran, and Michael Wachtel. (*Stanford Slavic Studies*, Volumes 29–30, Stanford, 2005).

I would like to thank David Brandenberger, who tracked down the original Kustodiev publications and carried out much of the scanning for the illustrations in chapter 5. Yulia Borisova, my graduate assistant, did a wonderful job pulling together the final manuscript from its separate pieces.

Finally, I have had great support from the people at the University of Washington Press, especially Michael Duckworth, and from REECAS, the Herbert J. Ellison Center for Russian, East European, and Central Asian Studies at the University of Washington's Jackson School of International Studies. Steve Hanson and Glennys Young helped put the project together, Sigrid Asmus did a superb editing job on the final manuscript, and the elegant design was provided by Ted Cotrotsos. Naturally, any errors that remain are mine.

Andrew Baruch Wachtel
Evanston, 2006

NOTE ON TRANSLITERATION

Throughout this book, Russian names are transliterated according to the Library of Congress system. The exceptions are that surnames ending in "skii" are transliterated as ending in "sky" (e.g., Rimsky-Korsakov, not Rimskii-Korsakov, Dostoevsky not Dostoevskii). In addition, names that are well-known in English according to other transliteration rules are rendered using their traditional forms (e.g., Tolstoy, Meyerhold, Diaghilev). When such names appear in titles of works in footnotes and/or in the list of works consulted, I use the Library of Congress form to make searching for these titles easier for the Russophone reader.

PLAYS OF EXPECTATIONS

Intertextual Relations in Russian Twentieth-Century Drama

INTRODUCTION

FROM THE PERSPECTIVE OF THE TWENTY-FIRST CENTURY, the last quarter of the twentieth century will undoubtedly be remembered as the time when theory, in multiple manifestations, dominated literary studies and the critical landscape. The field of Slavic languages and literatures has remained well behind the crest of the theoretical wave whose leading edge has been provided by specialists trained originally in English, French, and German. There is, however, one exception to this: intertextual studies. In this field, relatively unknown and underappreciated, Slavicists (and Slavic-born scholars) have developed two major lines of research. One, which grows out of Kiril Taranovsky's essays from the late 1960s and early 1970s on Osip Mandelstam, focuses on close readings of texts to elucidate the tangled web of intertextual connections that makes Russian poetry a "citational epic" (to quote the phrase of my colleague Ilya Kutik).[1] The other, which can be traced to Mikhail Bakhtin's musings on the nature of language, and their fleshing out in the work of Julia Kristeva (among others), sees intertextuality as a more or less universal phenomenon. This school is more interested in a theoretical understanding of the nature and range of possible intertextual relationships than in producing readings of individual works.[2] Both schools of thought share the conviction that the defining feature of literary texts is not, as Marxists and New Historicists of various stripes would have it, the interaction of texts with the external world, nor, as Deconstructionists would claim, the relationship of texts to language itself, but rather the interplay of text with text.

For both of the above camps, however, poetic texts have been the primary field of inquiry, with prose fiction taking second place. Such a focus makes sense, of course, because poetry, the most compressed of art forms, is also the one in which the role of intertextual dialogue among texts is most easily visible. Scholarly works that have examined this topic in relation to other art forms have, unfortunately, generally failed to address the issue of whether there is anything specific about the way intertextuality is employed outside the milieu of poetic and prose fictional dramas. Thus, in his otherwise excellent book *The Memory of Tiresias: Intertextuality and Film*, Mikhail Iampolski does not ask whether there is anything specific to the cinematic medium that would make its use in film qualitatively

3

different from its use in poetry and prose.

It has long been my belief that, at least in drama and theater, there are important ways in which the specificity of the medium impinges on and complicates intertextual practice. This is not to say that all varieties of intertextual usage in drama and theater are unique. Many of the effects produced by intertextual play are identical to those produced in better studied literary contexts. However, while the essays in this book frequently address those more traditional types of intertextuality, the focus here is on what might be called the varieties of intertextual experience that are specific to the dramatic and theatrical media. In particular, a number of the essays in this collection concern the fact that in the drama far more actors, and I use the word deliberately, are affected by intertextual usage and that their complex reactions to intertextual usages can make the experience of intertextuality in the theatrical context more complex and interesting than in non-performance media.

When, in the course of reading a poem, one recognizes the presence of material derived from some other literary source, the reaction is by nature an individual one. You have seen the connection, and its meaning (if you care to follow it up), depends primarily on your own reading experience. And of course, if you *don't* recognize the citation, then it simply does not exist for your reading of the poem. Even if you are a professional reader or critic who feels the need to try to reconstruct what the author of the poem might have wanted to say by including the cited word or words (and even if you do not believe in authorial intent and therefore choose to ascribe meaning here to "the text") you are engaged in a relatively solitary project. Whether or not you choose to link the voice of the lyric "I" (who is quoting) with that of the author, the intertextual dialogue is between you and the text, you and the tradition, or you and the author. In a novel, this dialogue can be made more complex because you need to pose a further question that is not generally asked of the poetic text: From whose per-spective does the quotation come? If it is from the narrator, then are the characters in the novel aware that they are part of an intertextual dialogue, or not? And if the intertextual reference is supplied by a character, do other characters perceive the intertextual play? Are they affected by it or is the intertextual connection to be made (if it is made at all) only by you, the reader behind the other characters' backs, as it were?

In drama (as in film, although that medium is considered only mini-mally in this book), the situation is far more complex. Because characters interact with each other in the drama far more directly than they do in fiction it is frequently the case that they produce and experience intertextual connections in a direct and obvious way. Thus, to use one primitive example, when Arkadina and Treplev exchange lines from *Hamlet* in *The Seagull*, they know quite consciously that they are doing so. The reader or spectator of the play probably, though not necessarily, also recognizes that *Hamlet* has been invoked. However, it is almost certain that the meaning of *Hamlet* for the characters and the reader of the play is not the same. What is more, in performance, it is crucial that the reaction or expectation of a spectator is not his or hers alone. Rather, it may well be affected by the reaction of neighbors or the audience as a whole. Thus, the relatively unsophisticated theatergoer may recognize, because of the reactions of his neighbor, that there is some kind of inside theatrical joke going on without being exactly aware of what it is. And while the percentage of theatergoers who would be familiar with and appreciate intertextual references to *Hamlet* is high, a far smaller number might recognize many other, more obscure references. The same can be said about the characters within a play, not all of whom necessarily recognize that what has just been said by a fellow character refers not only to their "real world" but also to a literary world lying outside the lives depicted on stage. To give an example that will appear again in one of the other chapters in this volume, if there is a character in Leo Tolstoy's play *The Living Corpse* who is named Anna Karenina (as there is), can we assume that all the characters in the play know what this name implies?

And of course, verbal intertexts are not the only kind available in theater. Thus, when a director asks an actor to make a gesture that mimics one made in another famous production (perhaps of an entirely different play), it is exceptionally difficult to unravel for whose benefit this is done. Clearly, an audience member who has seen the other production might be expected to appreciate the reference, which might well lead him or her to discover unexpected connections between the two plays in question even if there is no obvious thematic or verbal connection.[3] But are we to think that other characters in the play should recognize this gesture, as if they also had theatrical memory? Or are they to be understood as stuck permanently in the endless present of their performance, lacking any genre memory? Such questions become especially pertinent when, as is the case with *Petrushka*, considered in this volume, some of the relevant intertexts are drawn from performance rather than a text-based medium (as with the folk puppet theater or classical ballet). They are equally as true when we have to do with subtexts drawn from visual art (as considered in chapter 5 in the essay on *Lady Macbeth of Mtsensk*).

I do not wish to imply that there are any easy answers to the questions I have posed above. Rather, the series of essays that follows represents an attempt to describe and analyze a large variety of ways in which intertextual references were employed by Russian dramatists (in the broad sense of the word) in what can loosely be called the modernist period. Strictly speaking, however, this is not a book about modern Russian theater and drama. Rather, I have chosen to focus on works from a specific period and literary tradition as my test case primarily because the exceptional vitality of Russian twentieth-century theater makes it an excellent medium in which to find answers to the theoretical questions that have been posed in this introduction.

At this point, I should say a word about the essays. The work that appears here is my own, written over the course of the past fifteen years. Some essays have been published before, although they have generally been recast and modified for inclusion in this book. Not all the essays deal primarily with theatrical aspects of intertextuality. That is to say, some of what is presented here is text-based analysis. Nevertheless, I believe that each essay poses a specific theoretical problem that will be of interest to students of theater as well as to students of Russian culture and of intertextuality, and I hope that the book as a whole will serve as a starting point for a consideration of the particularities of dramatic and theatrical intertexuality.

NOTES

1. See Taranovsky. This pioneering work was followed up in the United States by Taranovsky's student Omry Ronen. Similar work was done in the Soviet Union by Garik Levinton and others. Kutik's ideas are developed in his essay "Tri veka russkoi poezii. Kakoi zhe iz nikh zolotoi" on the website www.russianpoetry.net. It may well be that the relative brevity of the modern Russian literary tradition encourages recognition and exploitation of textual interconnections. In comparison to other major literatures, the Russian tradition produced practically all its masterworks in a frenetic period of some 150 years from the early nineteenth to the late twentieth century.

2. In addition to the authors mentioned, the most thoroughgoing attempts to produce paradigmatic theories of intertextuality belong to the Russian expatriate critic Igor Smirnov and his German colleague at Konstanz, Renate Lachmann. Anglophone readers can sample her work in *Memory and Literature: Intertextuality in Russian Modernism*, 1997. Smirnov's terminologically dense considerations of intertextuality have not, unfortunately, been translated into English. Of course, Slavs and Slavists are by no means the only literary scholars working this particular field. Harold Bloom's heroic efforts to create an intertextual theory in *The Anxiety of Influence* comes to mind immediately.

3. For an excellent preliminary consideration of this phenomenon, see Marvin Carlson.

CHAPTER 1
Intertextual Clusters: *The Living Corpse* in Russian Culture

WHEN CHALLENGED TO EXPLAIN just what he did not like about Anton Chekhov's plays, Leo Tolstoy criticized them for their lack of "a knot, a center, from which everything and to which everything would flow."[1] The same complaint cannot be made about *The Living Corpse* (written 1900, first published 1911), the play that Tolstoy wrote in direct response to Chekhov's concept of drama.[2] It is clearly constructed around a central knot—the fake suicide of the main character, Fedia Protasov, and his "resurrection" as a "living corpse."

But it is not merely their centrality in the drama's plot that makes Fedia's acts a worthy subject for scholarly investigation in the context of dramatic intertextuality. More important is that the thematic knot formed by the act of fake suicide and subsequent "resurrection" has been of cardinal importance for Russian thought, and has appeared frequently (and with complicated variations) in Russian culture and society. Indeed, it would not be an exaggeration to say that this knot has been one of a handful of paradigms central to the development not just of Russian literature but of Russian history in general. For Tolstoy, and for his readers, Fedia's fake suicide recalled a panoply of heterogeneous subtexts. Fedia's act is, therefore, not simply the intratextual central point in the play, it is also the point to which intertextual meaning flows and from which Tolstoy engages his varied intertexts. Finally, in its turn, Tolstoy's version of the fake suicide plot became the central subtext for subsequent treatments of the theme in Russia. The purpose of this chapter, then, is to unravel the thematic knot of fake suicide, to demonstrate what Tolstoy might have been trying to say in using it, and to show how Tolstoy's broadening of the theme allowed it to be used in subsequent works of literature. Finally, it will, I hope, illustrate how intertextual thematic clusters evolve in a given tradition's cultural memory.

In *The Living Corpse*, the theme of fake suicide and subsequent resurrection draws extratextual meaning from at least four different kinds of intertexts: a real-life situation, literary texts by other authors, religious and philosophical concepts, and Tolstoy's own earlier work. Of course, the presence of intertextual material in *The Living Corpse* has been recognized by many scholars. But their analyses have not gone beyond attempts to prove that individual scenes and characters in the play had specific counterparts in preexisting texts.[3] My concern is somewhat different. Instead of looking at intertextual dialogues with individual works, I will be examining Tolstoy's "polylogue" with competing conceptions of a sociocultural theme. I believe that for Tolstoy, and for his implied reader, the play derives much of its meaning through the interaction of the central dramatic knot with its subtexts.

Real-life Intertexts in *The Living Corpse*

As readers of the play will recall, Fedia Protasov is a good-natured but weak-willed aristocrat married to Liza. At the beginning of the play we discover that, for the umpteenth time, Fedia has run off to the gypsies and squandered all the family money. Although she loves her husband, eventually, at the urging of her mother, Liza resolves to cut her ties with the irresponsible Fedia and to marry her longtime admirer, Viktor Karenin. For this, of course, she must obtain a divorce. But Fedia does not wish to subject himself to the demeaning lies that would be required to free his wife.[4] Instead, at the instigation of the gypsy woman, Masha, he decides to escape the impasse by faking suicide. He pretends to drown himself, and Viktor and Liza (who evidently really believe he has killed himself) are married. Everything goes awry, however, when Fedia's identity is discovered. All three characters are brought to trial, and when Fedia finally decides that there is no other way out of the situation he takes his own life.

The most obvious source for Protasov's fake suicide and the complications that flow from it was a real-life story well known both to Tolstoy and to a relatively large circle of Moscow society.[5] As the pertinent details of this case have been covered thoroughly in the Tolstoy literature, I will only provide a summary here.[6]

In 1881, E. P. Simon, the daughter of an acquaintance of Tolstoy's, married N. S. Gimer, a middle-ranking clerk in the Ministry of Justice. Gimer turned out to be a drunkard, and, after two years of marriage, having given birth to a son, E. P. Simon-Gimer left her husband. Her mother then introduced her to P. P. Akimov, a white-collar employee of the railroad. E. P. Simon-Gimer never divorced her first husband, but lived as Akimov's common-law wife for approximately seven years. Unfortunately it turned out that Akimov was no better than Gimer, and Simon-Gimer finally left him in 1890.[7] Sometime in the early '90s she met and fell in love with S. I. Chistov. Having resolved to marry Chistov, she attempted to get a divorce from her first husband, but for reasons that remain unclear the divorce was not granted. At this point Simon-Gimer became desperate. She paid her first husband to fake his own suicide. He pretended to drown himself, and the "widow" was soon remarried. However, the scheme was uncovered as soon as Gimer attempted to obtain a new passport. E. P. Simon-Gimer's second marriage was annulled, and she and her first husband were put on trial in 1897. The two were sentenced to Siberian exile, but, as a result of the intervention of high-placed friends, the sentence was commuted to a year in prison and then suspended.

Clearly, *The Living Corpse* parallels the Simon-Gimer story in a number of respects. Nevertheless, many crucial elements of the Simon-Gimer case do not correspond to the plot of Tolstoy's play. The most prominent changes include Liza's ignorance of the fact that Fedia's suicide is a sham, and a shift from the middle-class circles of Gimer-Simon to the upper-class society of the Protasovs and the Karenins. These and other differences have caused some critics to downplay the importance of the Simon-Gimer story for Tolstoy's drama.[8]

This, I believe, is a mistake. For Tolstoy's contemporaries, a mere hint would have been sufficient to call the notorious Simon-Gimer case to mind. The silent presence of this prototype would thus have lent Tolstoy's play the ring of truth he so valued in a work of art. In addition, Tolstoy could expect his audience to know just where and how his version of the story differed from the original. As a result, the real-life situation could serve as a kind of neutral ground (a control group, as it were) against which other intertexts would stand out in high relief. Finally, to turn to Tolstoy's own creative process for a moment, while the real-life prototype did not in the end provide either the plot or the characters of *The Living Corpse*, the Simon-Gimer story did call up a host of associations without which he might never have written the play. In particular, Gimer's fake suicide and its consequences echoed a number of literary texts in which a fake suicide was used as an important plot motif. Thus, the Simon-Gimer story served as a first step, the initial block of the intertextual foundation on which *The Living Corpse* was constructed.

Contemporary Literary Intertexts in *The Living Corpse*

The best-known literary text that the Simon-Gimer story called to mind was one to which Tolstoy had taken a violent dislike many years before: Nikolai Chernyshevsky's novel, *What Is to Be Done?* It should be noted that far from being an obscure text (as it might now seem to non-Russian readers), in Russia this novel was probably the most widely known work of the nineteenth century. As a contemporary put it: "In my sixteen years at the university I never did meet a student who had not read the famous novel while he was still in school . . . In this respect, the works, for example, of Ivan Turgenev or Ivan Goncharov—not to mention Nikolai Gogol or Aleksandr Pushkin—are far behind the novel *What Is to Be Done?*"[9] For Tolstoy, Chernyshevsky's work was something to be abused whenever possible, but it was to be used frequently as well.[10] There is one overt reference to the novel in *The Living Corpse*. In act 4, scene 1, part 5, Fedia is thinking about shooting himself when Masha the gypsy enters the room.

> MASHA (*grabbing the letter*). You wrote that you killed yourself, right? Not about the pistol? You wrote that you killed.
> FEDIA. Yes, that I would no longer exist.
> MASHA. Great, great, great. Did you ever read *What Is to Be Done?*
> FEDIA. I read it, I guess.
> MASHA. Well, it's a boring novel, but there's one very, very good thing there. He, what's his name, Rakhmanov, goes and pretends that he drowned himself.[11] (34:65)

However, the connections between *What Is to Be Done?* and *The Living Corpse* extend far beyond this scene. The general plot outlines of the two works are remarkably similar. Both center on a love triangle involving a woman and two men. In the novel and in the play the first and second husbands of the main female character are not strangers and rivals but friends. Indeed, in both cases the two men were friends even before the initial marriages. In both works, when it becomes apparent that the first marriage is unviable, the supplanted husband cedes his wife directly, and more or less willingly, to the second. Finally, in both cases, the first husband liberates his wife by faking suicide and disappearing.

There are a number of other details linking Protasov with Lopukhov, Liza with Vera Pavlovna, and Karenin with Kirsanov. Just before Masha convinces Fedia to fake his suicide, she sees a gun by his side and is convinced that he really intends to take his own life. She exclaims: "*Vot durak. Pravo, durak*" (34:62). ("What a fool. A real fool.") The first chapter of Chernyshevsky's novel, the chapter which describes Lopukhov's fake suicide, is entitled "*Durak*" (The Fool), and that is the "name" which all the people in the chapter give to the mysterious "suicide."

When Liza receives Fedia's suicide note (remember, she does not know that the suicide was a sham), she becomes hysterical, decides that she really loved only Fedia, and sends Karenin away (34:72). This scene exactly parallels the reaction of Vera Pavlovna when she receives Lopukhov's suicide note and temporarily banishes Kirsanov.[12] In both cases, however, the woman is speedily reconciled with and married to the second husband.

At the same time, there are extremely important areas in which the novel and the play diverge. These are not so much on the level of the plot, but rather on that of the plot's meaning; this becomes particularly obvious when we examine the outcome of the fake suicide in the two works. In *What Is to Be Done?* Kirsanov and Vera Pavlovna live happily ever after. Lopukhov eventually returns to Russia where, without any trouble, he passes for Charles Beaumont, the American employee of a British firm, marries the girl of his dreams, and gets back in contact with his old friends. The potential problems raised by Lopukhov/Beaumont's strangely split existence—that is, the question of how two individuals with overlapping but not identical personalities, psychologies, and life experiences manage to coexist in the same body—are not addressed. This character is able to retain some Lopukhov memories and personality traits, while conveniently sloughing off all aspects of his past that would be troubling for his Beaumont existence. For example, although it is true that he loved Vera Pavlovna and was a close friend of Kirsanov's, he was led to his fake suicide by feelings of bitterness toward both of them. After his return, however, he recalls only their former friendship and has evidently forgotten the acrimonious days before his disappearance. Nor, on a more quotidian plane, does the fact that he is still legally married to Vera Pavlovna prevent him from marrying Katia Polozova. In effect, Chernyshevsky allows Lopukhov/Beaumont to have the best of two lives without any of the problems that might conceivably plague this strange, hydralike being.

The questionable logic of Lopukhov's personal reincarnation is echoed on the novel's sociological level. Chernyshevsky believes that social transformation is right around the corner; the "new people" (of whom Lopukhov is one) will usher in a utopia similar to the one that Vera Pavlovna envisions in her famous fourth dream. Once again, however, the problem of the connection between the old order and the new is never seriously addressed.[13] Nor is the mechanism for passing from one to the other revealed overtly. The reader is evidently meant to believe that change will occur swiftly, but without the use of force, as a result of the dictates of logic. In fact, however, a closer examination of the text indicates that Chernyshevsky conceived this mechanism in religious terms. In this regard, it is crucial that Lopukhov's reappearance is described in terms that link him directly with Christ.[14] Christ, of course, as man/God, handles a double identity (before and after his crucifixion) without any difficulty. Evidently, Lopukhov/Beaumont, in his imitation of Christ, is meant to function as a kind of metonym for Chernyshevsky's model for the revolutionary transformation of Russian society in general. The fake suicide motif is therefore linked on the one hand to questions of revolution, and on the other, to the problem of resurrection.[15]

For Tolstoy, Chernyshevsky's resolution of the fake suicide plot must have seemed glib to the point of puerility. Long before he wrote *The Living Corpse*, Tolstoy had come to the conclusion that the problem of resurrection was not primarily physical, but rather philosophical. In the play, once he becomes reincarnated as a "living corpse," Protasov is unable to figure out who he is, or how to reconcile the radical break between his past and present selves; that is, he is neither able to forget his past completely and start afresh, nor is he able, like Lopukhov, to integrate selected parts of his past with his present condition. While Tolstoy accepts Chernyshevsky's linkage of personal and social transformation, he turns the argument on its head. Just as Protasov is unable to take on a new identity after his resurrection, so society is unwilling or unable to modify its rigid attitudes toward marriage and divorce in the face of his actions. In prosecuting Protasov, Liza, and Karenin, the judicial system reveals a fatal inability to reconcile law and justice. At the same time, Tolstoy eliminates the parallels between his resurrected hero and Christ that underlie Chernyshevsky's novel. Ultimately then, *The Living Corpse* can be seen as a parody of *What Is to Be Done?* in the sense that it uses the same literary material in order to radically reevaluate it.[16]

If Chernyshevsky's novel served primarily as a model to be rebutted, a different Russian literary text used the fake suicide theme in a way that was probably more to Tolstoy's liking: Aleksandr Sukhovo-Kobylin's "comedy-joke," *Tarelkin's Death*.[17] As in *What Is to Be Done?* and *The Living Corpse*, a fake suicide forms the central plot element in *Tarelkin's Death*. In this case, Tarelkin, a petty thieving bureaucrat, fakes suicide in order to avoid his creditors and to extort money from his corrupt superior, Varravin. However, Varravin uncovers Tarelkin's scheme and, after a series of grotesquely funny machinations, forces the now identity-less Tarelkin to make his miserable way in the world, literally from nothing.

Two themes in *Tarelkin's Death* are important for *The Living Corpse* but were absent or only latently present in the Simon-Gimer case and in *What Is to Be Done?*: the first is a sharp parody of the criminal justice system, and the second is an overt concern with questions of death, resurrection, and personal identity.[18]

Sukhovo-Kobylin's bitter satire was considered so inflammatory that, although the play was published in 1869, it could not be staged until 1900.[19] The playwright portrays a judicial system (and particularly a police system) that is rotten to the core. Officials are either too stupid to understand what is happening around them or so venal that they can easily be bought off. The scenes in *Tarelkin's Death* in which the police interrogate the "resurrected" Tarelkin play out a grotesque version of the senseless and tragic situation that Tolstoy describes in act 6 of *The Living Corpse*.

More central, however, is the contrast between the consequences of the fake suicide in the two plays. After his supposed death, Tarelkin takes on the identity of his former neighbor, Sila Silych Kopylov. Unfortunately for him, it turns out that Kopylov has also died and, when this fact is discovered, the "resurrected" Tarelkin is left without any identity at all:

RASPLIUEV. There's no doubt about it. Kopylov died. Died of apoplexy! Died in the village of Do-Nothing, was cut open, and buried in the ground!! (*Whacks a piece of paper*)
VARRAVIN. How horrible!
RASPLIUEV. And now this again. Tarelkin died! He died—and he was buried in the ground by me!! (*Strikes his chest*)—by me!!! And now this 'un: Who is he?!!
VARRAVIN. Hold on! I know who he is! It's . . . it's life's greatest peril – . . . Listen to me . . . Do you know what a werewolf is?[20]

Tarelkin, raised from the dead, becomes at one and the same time two people and no one. His situation is, in effect, exactly the opposite of that of Lopukhov/Beaumont.[21] Tarelkin retains only the unnecessary traits of his former existence, and is unable to take on those of his "new" incarnation.

> TARELKIN. What can I say?—I told you—I'm Kopylov.
> RASPLIUEV. You're lying, you devilish soul! He died. Here are the papers (*to Kachala*). Twist his arm!
> TARELKIN. Oy-oy-oy,—well O.K., I'm Tarelkin—oy, Tarelkin!
> RASPLIUEV (*forcefully*). You're lying—Tarelkin—Why General Varravin himself—what are you wasting my time for, anathema (*to Kachala*) Twist!
> TARELKIN. O gods, ay . . . I'm . . . I'm . . . both of them.
> VARRAVIN (*To Raspliuev*). And both of them are dead.[22]

In many respects, Fedia Protasov's position after his fake suicide is similar.

> FEDIA. But I don't exist.
> PETUSHKOV. What do you mean, "don't exist"?
> FEDIA. Don't exist. I'm a corpse. That's right. (34:78)

Like Tarelkin, like Lopukhov, Fedia simultaneously does and does not exist in the real world. But, whereas Lopukhov is able to forge ahead, to become resurrected as a living being, Tarelkin and Fedia Protasov fail to reconcile their "before" and "after" identities. As Fedia puts it: "I'm a corpse and you can't do anything to me; there's no position worse than mine" (34:93). Still, there is a crucial difference between the situations of Fedia and Tarelkin/Kopylov. Tarelkin is a cheat and an extortionist, and while there is a certain abstract tragedy in his final situation, the spectator essentially does not care what happens to this grotesquely comic character. But Fedia and his situation are perceived as genuinely tragic. Despite his resurrection, Fedia remains the identical person.[23] He is still the same weak-willed, good-hearted, ineffectual drunkard he was before. Now, however, these traits cannot save him, and the logic of his position leads inexorably to his real death. Thus, as was the case with *What Is to Be Done?*, it seems that Tolstoy evoked a literary subtext as a source of parody.

The same sorts of situations reappear, but they are evaluated differently.

Tolstoy broke with his literary predecessors not in his use of the fake suicide theme, but in regard to the subsequent fate of the resurrected "suicide." His purpose in recalling early texts was polemical; by reusing and reevaluating the same theme, Tolstoy emphasizes what separates his ideas from those of his forebears. Yet while literary texts are clearly vitally important for understanding the meaning of the fake suicide theme in *The Living Corpse*, they were by no means the only ones that would have come to Tolstoy's mind and to the thoughts of his readers when the subject of resurrection was broached. In 1881, during one of his extended visits to Moscow, Tolstoy became acquainted with the librarian of the Rumiantsev Museum. The two men evidently became quite friendly, and saw each other frequently whenever Tolstoy was in Moscow. The man's name was Nikolai Fedorovich Fedorov. As it turned out, in addition to being a librarian he was a strikingly original philosopher. One of the core beliefs of Fedorov's philosophical system was the necessity for mankind to harness the powers of nature and science in order to accomplish the actual physical resurrection of all those who had ever lived on earth. The accomplishment of this task was, in Fedorov's view, the prerequisite for creating the kingdom of heaven on earth. "Christianity believes in the triumph over death; but that belief is dead and that is why death exists; that belief will remain dead as long as it remains separated from all of mankind's other forces, that is, until all the forces of all people join together for the general goal of resurrection."[24]

Fedorov's ideas, particularly those concerning resurrection, struck a chord with many Russian thinkers of the second half of the nineteenth century. Fedor Dostoevsky, for example, speaking for himself and for the philosopher Vladimir Solov'ev, wrote a letter to Fedorov's chief disciple, N. P. Peterson, in which he expressed the hope that Fedorov understood the resurrection of mankind literally and not allegorically.[25] It is perhaps not surprising that Dostoevsky was attracted to Fedorov's ideas, particularly since there is some evidence that he saw his own life in terms of a pattern of death and resurrection. It will be recalled that Dostoevsky was officially sentenced to death for his part in the so-called Petrashevsky affair, and that he was actually led out to be executed before it was announced that his sentence and those of his comrades had been commuted.[26] After this symbolic death Dostoevsky spent the next four years in prison. The last line of his autobiographical novel describing these years, *Notes from the House of the Dead*, may be taken to indicate Dostoevsky's own view of the experience: "Freedom, new life, resurrection from the dead . . . What a glorious moment!"[27]

Tolstoy was also well aware of Fedorov's philosophy, as is demonstrated by a letter he wrote to V. I. Alekseev in November 1881. "He [Fedorov] has formulated a plan for the general affairs of all humankind, which has as its goal the resurrection of all people in the flesh. First of all, it's not as crazy as it seems (Don't be afraid, I never did and do not now share his views, but I understand them so well that I feel myself able to defend them against the claims of all other beliefs having an external goal)."[28] Tolstoy undoubtedly knew that Fedorov's plan to resurrect the molecules of the dead was crazy. But he liked the librarian because he lived what he preached—celibacy, asceticism, vegetarianism, and so forth, all of which Tolstoy advocated but was himself unable to practice consistently.

But on a more theoretical level, what bothered Tolstoy about Fedorov's ideas was that in Fedorov's belief resurrection would automatically lead to transformation. Like Chernyshevsky, Fedorov never seems to wonder about why and how the moral transformation of mankind will be effected. Evidently, as far as he is concerned, the physical fact of general resurrection ensures a remaking of the world for the better. As we will see, however, for Tolstoy the act of resurrection is not social but personal, and a positive outcome for the process is by no means guaranteed. Thus, the Fedorov subtext is also invoked in *The Living Corpse*. But Tolstoy does not parody it as he does other literary texts. Instead, by concentrating on the failure of resurrection in the case of an individual, Tolstoy calls Fedorov's excessively optimistic system into question.

Tolstoyan Intertexts in *The Living Corpse*

Although a recognition of Tolstoy's use of the intertexts cited above is vital to an understanding of *The Living Corpse*, another group of texts plays an even more important role in the play: Tolstoy's own earlier works. Tolstoy used the theme of death and resurrection frequently throughout his career. One might recall, for example, Prince Andrei's near death and subsequent resurrection at the battle of Austerlitz and then again at Borodino in *War and Peace* (completed in 1869), as well as Pierre Bezukhov's moral death and resurrection in the same novel. Tolstoy's late novel, *Resurrection* (1899), is obviously built around this theme, one that evidently had an autobiographical dimension as well: Tolstoy's *Confession* (1881) is structured around it (as, of course, are many confessions since Augustine). However, the work in which death and resurrection is featured most prominently, and the work that is most important for *The Living Corpse*, is *Anna Karenina* (completed in 1877).

As is the case with the non-Tolstoyan texts discussed previously, the existence of a connection between Tolstoy's play and his earlier novel has been noted by critics. It could hardly have been missed, considering that Liza's second husband is Viktor Karenin (not Anna's Aleksei, but close enough) and his mother's name is Anna Karenina. Of course, Tolstoy did occasionally recycle character names innocently—Nekhliudov comes to mind immediately[29]—but the choice of the name Karenin here was certainly not accidental.

In an article entitled "A Real-Life Story and a Literary Plot," A. Mariamov demonstrates a number of ways in which *The Living Corpse* can be seen as a commentary on *Anna Karenina*. In Mariamov's view, the resurrection of Anna in the person of Viktor's mother, a society woman *comme il faut* in all the wrong ways, indicates yet another attempt by Tolstoy to reject his early work. "To revive his former heroine merely in order to afflict her with senile amnesia and to force her to forget the most searing moments of her own life—that is indeed a horrible vengeance. The only thing that could have brought Tolstoy to this kind of vengeance was a stubborn conviction which forced him, in a cruel battle with himself, to reject his earlier book . . ."[30]

While certain aspects of Mariamov's interpretation are appealing, I believe that it is impossible to characterize the relationship between these two works in particular, and between the artistic work of the "early" and "late" Tolstoy in general, as one of simple rejection. As I demonstrated in an earlier article, the plot of *Anna Karenina* can be seen as revolving around the figurative deaths and resurrections of all four main characters.[31] There are, however, two very different outcomes to this process. The deaths and resurrections of Kitty and Levin occur in a context of Christianity. They lead to moral regeneration, and, ultimately, to new life and happiness. Those of Vronsky and Anna are in a pagan context and lack a moral/religious component. After their respective resurrections, neither Anna nor Vronsky choose the path of redemption, and eventually they are condemned to despair and new death.[32]

Most critics who have written on *The Living Corpse* find Fedia to be a sympathetic character, primarily because of his rejection of bourgeois values.[33] In fact, Fedia is a far more ambivalent figure. While it is true that he abhors the false values of his class and has a number of admirable qualities, he is also untrustworthy, a drunkard, and a spendthrift. Most damning of all, when he is given the chance to be reborn, a chance that opens up the possibility of moral regeneration even to Tolstoy's greatest sinners, he fails. This failure is illustrated by his actions after his resurrection. Fedia evidently rejects the pure and disinterested love of Masha the gypsy (an act that mirrors his rejection of his loving wife before the fake suicide), even though by his actions he has already made life among the gypsies untenable for her. In addition, he is arrested only because he cannot resist narrating his melodramatic history while drunk in a public place.

In his failure to recognize his death and resurrection as an invitation to moral regeneration, Fedia strongly resembles Vasilii Kuzmich Aristidov in the story "Zhivoi mertvets" (The Living Dead Man) by Prince Vladimir Odoevsky. This tale undoubtedly figures as another literary subtext for the drama, and it may well have provided the idea for the title of Tolstoy's play.[34] The story describes the posthumous wanderings of Aristidov, who discovers that all those who had seemingly respected him in his lifetime had actually despised him, and that his moral failings led to disaster for his family. In the end, it turns out that the whole story was merely a nightmare. When Aristidov wakes up (his figurative resurrection) he quickly shakes off the impressions of the dream, and we realize that it will in no way cause him to turn over a new moral leaf. In this respect, Aristidov can be considered a forbear of Anna, Vronsky, and Fedia, with the difference that Odoevsky does not provide any ultimate punishment for him in the story.[35]

Like Tarelkin in Sukhovo-Kobylin's play, and like Gimer in real life, Fedia loses his identity after his fake suicide and is unable to gain a new one after his "resurrection." Death and resurrection do not result in Fedia's spiritual renewal as they manifestly do for Kitty and Levin, Nekhliudov and Pierre, all of whom find their "true" identity as a result of this process. On the contrary, after his false suicide—his figurative death—he chooses the way of Vronsky and Anna. In Tolstoy's moral and literary universe, this path must inevitably lead to his real death, which comes by suicide in the final scene of the play. Thus, if any character in *The Living Corpse* can be said to represent a resurrected Anna Karenina, that character is surely

Fedia Protasov. At the same time, Protasov lives not just by and in himself and in the reflected light of Anna, but in varying relations to Gimer, Tarelkin, Lopukhov, and all of Tolstoy's other resurrected personages. Fedia is composed of bits and pieces of them all, a confused sum of heterogeneous parts.

Thus, *The Living Corpse* draws its meaning through an ingenious juxtaposition of a varied group of subtexts. Tolstoy uses the plot element of fake suicide to comment on the way that theme had previously been used in Russian culture. At the same time, he greatly broadens the philosophical implications of this plot element by emphasizing its potentially tragic aspects and by integrating it with one of his favorite topics: death and resurrection. Thus, fake suicide and death and resurrection become part of a single theme cluster that is further complicated by questions surrounding the resurrected character's tragic loss of identity. As a result, Fedia's fake suicide really becomes the "central knot" from which and to which everything flows; that is, it makes *The Living Corpse* a true drama in Tolstoyan terms.

The Literary Heirs of *The Living Corpse*

Tolstoy's play marks an apotheosis of the fake suicide in Russian literature. Moreover, this Tolstoyan theme cluster remained of central importance for the future course of Russian literary and cultural development, and its presence in a number of later works proves it to have been as resilient as the living corpses whose deaths (and lives) it described. While few subsequent works made use of all the potential inherent in the cluster, at least three important treatments of it, found in Russian literature of the 1920s and '30s, should be considered. Two are dramas: Vladimir Maiakovsky's *Klop* (*The Bedbug*, 1928), and Nikolai Erdman's *Samoubiitsa* (*The Suicide*, 1930). The third is a novel: Vladimir Nabokov's *Otchaianie* (*Despair*, 1936).

At first glance, *The Bedbug* seems to lack the fake suicide theme entirely, although in many other respects it clearly represents a revised version of *The Living Corpse*. Actually, a closer look reveals that Maiakovsky's play contains not one, but three versions of the fake or unsuccessful suicide. The first is comic, and it relates to Prisypkin's attempt to remake himself from Soviet worker to NEP-era bourgeois. In acts 1 and 2 we discover that he has changed his name from Ivan Prisypkin to the more impressive (to his ears anyway) Pierre Skripkin. A second is the attempted suicide of Zoia Berezkina, the spurned girlfriend of the play's hero, Prisypkin. At the end of act 2 she shoots herself in the breast, and there is nothing to lead the reader to believe that the shot was not fatal. But it turns out that Zoia only wounded herself, and she is still very much alive in the second part of the play, which takes place fifty years in the future. And Prisypkin's own death is also a kind of suicide, since it occurs as the result of a fire caused by excessive drinking.

In the second part of the play, Prisypkin is resurrected (the word is actually used a number of times in the text) through a process that may very well be derived from Fedorov.[36] Once Prisypkin is back on his feet, Maiakovsky follows Tolstoy in combining the death and resurrection theme with problems of personal identity. Indeed, after his resurrection, Prisypkin finds himself in a predicament close to that of Fedia Protasov. Like Fedia, he retains his old identity intact, despite the intervening fifty years. Unfortunately, his surroundings, and therefore the expectations of others, have changed radically during that time. Trapped in his old identity, Prisypkin can do nothing but agree to become an exhibit at the local zoo, a living corpse whose anachronistic presence recalls bygone days for the people of the future.

Erdman's play uses the fake-suicide theme quite openly. It will be recalled that the play's central figure, Semen Semenovich Podsekal'nikov decides to commit suicide because, to use an anachronistic term, he is unable to "find himself" in Soviet society. When news of his decision leaks out, various disaffected groups and individuals ask him to support their causes by claiming, in his suicide note, to have killed himself because of their concerns.[37] In exchange, they agree to bury him with great pomp and to support his wife and mother-in-law. Being weak-willed, Podsekal'nikov agrees to each of their mutually exclusive requests, but then finds himself unable to go through with the act. In the play's climactic scene, which takes place in the cemetery where Podsekal'nikov is to be buried, the hero rises from his open coffin. Podsekal'nikov's comic speech masks but does not entirely conceal the philosophical implications of his resurrection. In this case, the result is seemingly positive—through his fake suicide Podsekal'nikov has come to realize the value of his and any other individual human life: "Comrades, I don't want to die: not for you, not for them, not for a class, not for all humankind, and not for Maria Lukianovna. In life you may be my relatives, my loved ones, my close friends. But in the face of death what could be closer, more lovable, or more related than your own hand, foot, and stomach."[38] Of course, the tragedy implicit in Erdman's play is that Podsekal'nikov comes to his realization precisely at a time when Soviet society as a whole had lost all appreciation for the individual human life.

Finally, the fake-suicide theme is given a number of new twists in Vladimir Nabokov's *Despair*. Nabokov combines the theme cluster of fake suicide, resurrection, and loss of personal identity, with the theme of the double (or fake double), and that of murder. While on a business trip, the narrator, Herman, meets a man whom he takes to be his double. For various reasons, he conceives a plan whereby he will murder this double and then disappear. His wife will collect the insurance money due after his untimely death, and then he will be "resurrected" in some other country where she will rejoin him. The fake suicide and subsequent resurrection plot is cleverly combined with questions of personal identity. Is the double really a double? As it turns out, the two men do not look alike. But then why is it that Herman thinks they do? In addition, it is quite clear that Herman has gone insane and that the narrative we are reading is the work of a madman. This, naturally, leads the reader to wonder about the relationship between the pre-fake-suicide Herman, and his post-fake-suicide "double"—that is, his own insane reincarnation. Nabokov's novel represents a most complicated development of the fake suicide thematic cluster.

While the thematic knot of suicide (or fake suicide) and resurrection plays an important role in each of the three twentieth-century works discussed above, still another work, a novel in many ways emblematic of the course of Soviet cultural development, develops this knot with almost incredible virtuosity; I have in mind *Master i Margarita (The Master and Margarita)*, by Mikhail Bulgakov. The novel is far too complicated to analyze in depth here, but for my purposes it will suffice to recall that it is built around at least two parallel plots. One is set in Moscow in the 1920s and '30s and concerns a writer, the Master, who has produced a novel about Pontius Pilate. The other is a retelling of Christ's passion. Whether or not the version of the passion presented here is identical with the text of the master's novel is left ambiguous. Although the resurrection of Christ is not actually described in *The Master and Margarita*, it is of course unavoidably present in any reader's subconscious, and it therefore forms a strong subtext for the "modern" sections of the novel in which themes of death and resurrection are developed in complicated and original ways.

When we first see the Master, he is in an insane asylum; he has been committed, symbolically at least, for two types of attempted suicide. The first involves his attempt to publish his novel. We are told that the Master, despite having been clearly informed by the editorial board of a Moscow publishing committee that his book was unacceptable ideologically (not surprising in the officially atheistic Soviet Union of the late '20s and early '30s), nevertheless submitted his book elsewhere and even succeeded in finding a journal editor willing to publish excerpts. In the Soviet Union of this period such an act was tantamount to literary suicide, and, by the mid-'30s (*The Master and Margarita* was written from 1929 to 1940) could and sometimes did lead to an author's actual death. In the novel, the appearance of the Master's work leads to a vicious campaign against him for "printing an apology for Jesus Christ" and "Pilatism."[39] These attacks lead the Master to a second act of suicide (spiritual in this case); he burns all the copies of his manuscript. Summarizing the experience for his neighbor in the insane asylum, the Master emphasizes his connection with the living corpse theme: "I went out into the world holding it [the novel] in my hands, and that is when my life ended."[40]

Toward the end of the novel, however, both of these suicidal acts are redeemed by resurrections engineered by Woland (Satan) and Margarita, the Master's mistress. The novel is reconstituted by Woland's will, and at Margarita's request she and the Master are reunited. Their reunion, however, is evidently accompanied by their physical death (the nurse in the insane asylum tells the Master's neighbor that he has died and the neighbor predicts Margarita's death), and the novel's final scene depicts their transfiguration to the otherworldly tranquility they have earned by their earthly sufferings.

Although this concentration of suicide, death, and resurrection in the text of the novel is remarkable in and of itself, what makes *The Master and Margarita* emblematic of the Soviet period as a whole, as well as illustrating the centrality of this thematic knot for Russian culture, is the literary fate of the author and his text. Bulgakov was, for all intents and purposes, gradually hounded out of Soviet literature in the 1930s. *The Master and Margarita* was written, as they said in the Soviet Union, "for the desk drawer," since the author knew, even if his hero did not, that even to try to publish such a novel in the Stalinist era was unthinkable.[41] After Bulgakov's death in 1940, the novel remained unpublished and unknown until 1966, when the first part was published in the journal *Moskva*. As one of Bulgakov's biographers has said, "The novel's appearance created a sensation and *Moskva* was sold out immediately.... It was *The Master and Margarita* which overnight made Bulgakov's reputation."[42] Thus, by a quirk of history, the novel's fate turned out to have been encoded in its text.

Bulgakov's rise from the literary scrap heap marked the beginning of a process of ever-accelerating literary "resurrections" in the late Soviet and immediate post-Soviet period. Indeed, the words that Woland uses when he reconstitutes the Master's novel—"manuscripts don't burn"[43]—can be seen as emblematic of post-Soviet literary existence. The same logic applies to the ideas of social and political figures, and political scientists might do well to wonder whether the peculiar but widespread Russian fascination with and acceptance of the idea of posthumous rehabilitation in all areas of civic life is related to the strength of the living corpse theme in Russian culture. Fortunately, the fate of resurrected works and ideas in post-Soviet Russia has not resembled that of Tolstoy's hero. Unlike Fedor Protasov, who was unable to find a new identity after his resurrection, these works have had a powerful impact on the development of contemporary Russian literature, and have created a new generation of scholars, both Western and Russian, whose view of the literary process and the canon has been permanently altered by the reappearance of these literary "living corpses."

NOTES

1. The full quote is as follows: "[Tolstoy] began to develop the idea that drama is a special type of literature which has its own specific laws, that drama must have a central knot, a center from which everything and to which everything would flow, and that this does not exist in Chekhov at all" (Elpat'evsky, p. 144). The feeling that every true work of art must possess a single central core had evidently been part of Tolstoy's philosophy since at least the 1870s. In a letter to Strakhov, for example, Tolstoy remarked: "We need people who would show the senselessness of the search for thoughts in a work of art and who would constantly guide readers through the endless labyrinth of linkages that make up the stuff of art, and to the laws that serve as the basis of those linkages." L. N. Tolstoy, 62:269.

   Further citations from the work of Tolstoy in this book will be made by reference to volume and page number(s) of this edition. All translations are my own.

2. On 27 January, 1900, Tolstoy wrote the following entry in his diary: "Went to see

Uncle Vanya and became incensed. Decided to write a drama, *Corpse*. Jotted down a plan" (54:10).

3. Some of the more important works in this area include the commentary to *The Living Corpse* by S. D. Balukhatyi and V. S. Mishin in volume 34 of the 90-volume Tolstoy edition; see also Lakshin, pp. 381–430; Poliakova, pp. 219–319; and Mariamov, pp. 89–122.

4. Under nineteenth-century Russian law, in order to receive a divorce with the right to remarry, the innocent party had to prove (or the guilty one to admit) adultery. Thus, for Liza to remarry, Fedia would have had to confess to being an adulterer. And while Tolstoy presents him as a man with many flaws, betraying his wife sexually is not among them. It is, therefore, not surprising that he was loath to take the legal steps necessary to free her. Aleksei Karenin runs into the identical problem when asked to give Anna a divorce in *Anna Karenina*. It was also the central subject of a well-known play of Tolstoy's day, *Vtoraia molodost'* (Second Youth) by the now forgotten dramatist P. M. Nevezhin (1841–1919). Nevezhin's play was produced to great success at the Maly theatre in St. Petersburg in 1887, and was published in 1901 in the second volume of Nevezhin's two-volume collected works.

5. Tolstoy evidently first heard about the story from his friend, N. V. Davydov, the President of the Moscow Circuit Court. Davydov described Tolstoy's reaction to the story in an article entitled "*Iz vospominanii o L. N. Tolstom.*" See Davydov, 1911.

6. A more detailed description of the case can be found in volume 34 of the 90 volume Tolstoy edition, pp. 533–534.

7. She evidently made attempts to leave Akimov for a number of years before 1890. In 1887 her mother told Tolstoy the whole sad story. Tolstoy's characteristic but not very helpful advice was that "she must live with the husband with whom she is living, loving him as much as she is able and allowing him the possibility of being good to her. And she should leave him only when he tells her directly to leave" (64:101).

8. "It is as useless to search for the characteristics of Liza Protasov in the person of E. P. Gimer as it is to search for the prototype of Fedor in the man who was actually tried for being a 'living corpse' " (Mariamov, p. 101).

9. The quote is from a pamphlet by P. P. Tsitovich. It is cited in Paperno, p. 28.

10. In his unfinished comedy, *Zarazhennoe semeistvo* (*The Infected Family*), Tolstoy parodied Chernyshevsky and *What Is to Be Done?* Although in the 1890s he did have a few good things to say about Chernyshevsky's aesthetic program, Tolstoy's attitude toward Chernyshevsky's fiction remained negative to the very end. In 1910 he told Gusev, "I always found Chernyshevsky and his writings unpleasant" (Gusev, p. 223).

11. Masha's recollection of the name of the character in *What Is to Be Done?* who fakes suicide is, of course, incorrect: she should have said Lopukhov. Her use of the name Rakhmanov instead is extremely suggestive. Clearly the reader or spectator is supposed to realize that she "wanted" to say Rakhmetov (one of the other heroes of *What Is to Be Done?*). The name Rakhmanov does not appear in the novel. It is, however, the maiden name of Fedia's wife, Liza. Masha's Freudian slip hints at her hope that Fedia will, in a figurative sense, kill his wife through the act of fake suicide, and thereby be free to marry again.

12. Chernyshevsky, p. 11.

13. One of the remarkable things about Vera Pavlovna's fourth dream (which describes

the perfect future society) is its blithe combination of existing elements of social, material, and political life with ones that do not yet and may never exist.

14. When Vera Pavlovna hears that Lopukhov has returned she says to Kirsanov: "It is Easter today, Sasha, so say to Katenka: Verily he is risen" (Chernyshevsky, p. 332). For a thorough discussion of Chernyshevsky's use of religious imagery in *What Is to Be Done?*, see Paperno, pp. 195–218.

15. For Tolstoy's readers (and possibly for Tolstoy himself, although there is no evidence that he knew this work) the connection between fake suicide and revolutionary activity was strengthened by the appearance in 1897 of a novel called *Ovod* (originally written and published in 1896 in English under the title, *The Gadfly*) by one E. L. Voinich. In Voinich's novel the main character fakes suicide in order to disappear and embark on a career as a professional revolutionary. Voinich was an Englishwoman who was married to a Polish/Russian revolutionary. She translated from Russian to English, and there can be no doubt but that she borrowed the fake suicide motif from Chernyshevsky (whose novel any self-respecting Russian revolutionary knew by heart). Interestingly, in keeping with its epigonic Russian thematics, the novel proved much more popular in Russian than in English. In fact, it remained a classic in the Soviet Union, having been through fifty-seven Russian editions between 1897 and 1958, not to mention five stage versions and several movies.

16. This idea of parody represents a development of the definition proposed by Tynianov: "the parody of a tragedy will be a comedy . . . the parody of a comedy can be a tragedy" (p. 416).

17. Tolstoy never actually mentions Sukhovo-Kobylin's play, but, in addition to the connections that will be discussed below, there is a strange coincidence that could have encouraged Tolstoy to think about Sukhovo-Kobylin in connection with *The Living Corpse*. In 1850, when Sukhovo-Kobylin was a young man, he was accused of arranging the murder of his mistress. The case was a cause célèbre at the time, and Tolstoy wrote two letters about it to his aunt (See the 90 volume edition, 59:64, 81). The last name of the murdered mistress (which Tolstoy mentions several times) was Simon. This, of course, is the same name as the real-life prototype for Liza in *The Living Corpse*.

18. Of course, both of these themes were old favorites of Tolstoy's, but Sukhovo-Kobylin's play might well have helped him to see how they could be used in a dramatic work. It is, perhaps, not coincidental that Tolstoy was writing *The Living Corpse* just as *Tarelkin's Death* was about to be staged for the first time.

19. In both Imperial Russia and the Soviet Union, there were two levels of censorship for theatrical works. A play could be published if it passed the regular censorship but it could only be staged if approved by a second, more stringent, censorship committee.

20. Sukhovo-Kobylin, p. 256.

21. Interestingly enough, in Varravin's last line above, Sukhovo-Kobylin brings up a folkloric subtext that Tolstoy fails to actualize in *The Living Corpse*: the Russian tradition of vampirism. According to Slavic folk belief, suicides commonly turn into vampires who "lie in their graves as *undecayed corpses*." (emphasis mine) (Oinas, p. 112). According to Oinas (p. 111) the words for werewolf and vampire are frequently interchangeable.

22. Sukhovo-Kobylin, pp. 258–259.

23. This is symbolized by the fact that, unlike Lopukhov and Tarelkin, Fedia does not receive a new name after his resurrection.

24. Fedorov, 2:203–204. From the above citation it might be imagined that Fedorov meant resurrection to be understood metaphorically. However, from a number of his other articles it is clear that he meant the project to be conceived quite literally. See, for example, the article entitled, "*Roditeli i voskresiteli*," 2:273–274. For a general introduction to Fedorov's thought, see Lukashevich.

25. Dostoevsky, 30:13–15.

26. Actually, the sentence was never really to death, but it had been decided to teach the prisoners a lesson by making them believe that it was. For a detailed discussion of the mock execution and its aftermath see Frank, pp. 49–70.

27. Dostoevsky, 4:232. Of course, Dostoevsky uses the same paradigm of prison as a locus for resurrection in the epilogue of *Crime and Punishment*.

28. Tolstoy, 63:80–81. For a detailed discussion of Tolstoy's views on Fedorov, see Nikitin, 123–130. Dostoevsky and Tolstoy were by no means the only Russian intellectuals interested in Fedorov. In the area of science, for example, it was Fedorov who convinced his protégé, later recognized as the father of Soviet rocketry, K. I. Tsiolkovsky, of the need for space travel. As Viktor Shklovsky puts it: "He [Fedorov] dreamed of the physical resurrection of the dead, and was already worried about where to put resurrected mankind. That is why he considered it necessary to settle the stars" (Shklovsky, p. 448).

29. Characters by the name of Nekhliudov appear in "Notes of a Billiard Marker" (1855), "A Landowner's Morning" (1856), "Youth" (1857), "Lucerne" (1857), and in *Resurrection* (1899). It does not appear, however, that readers are expected to connect these various Nekhliudovs with each other.

30. Mariamov, p. 117.

31. See A. Wachtel, 1989.

32. Richard Gustafson discusses the theology of resurrection in Tolstoy's work. He believes that resurrection is one of the important methods whereby a Tolstoyan character goes from being a "Stranger" to being a "Resident." The latter category is, in Gustafson's vocabulary, a sort of ideal state of wholeness. "With resurrection, one becomes a Resident" (p. 51). What Gustafson does not recognize, it seems to me, is that resurrection does not always produce this kind of transformation in the works of Tolstoy. Sometimes, as is the case with Fedia, the Stranger remains a Stranger despite the potential for healing inherent in the process of resurrection.

33. See, for example, Lakshin, p. 397, and Poliakova, pp. 247–250.

34. Although the phraseology "*zhivoi trup*" may have been used in common parlance, the earliest literary use of this exact phrase that I have found is in Pushkin's 1836 poem "*Podrazhanie Italianskomu*" (An Imitation of the Italian). There the body of Judas is described as having been taken off the tree from which he hanged himself by a devil who "*brosil trup zhivoi v gortan' geeny gladnoi*" (threw the living corpse into hell's hungry maw). (*Pushkin, Polnoe sobranie sochinenii*, vol. 3, pt. 1, p. 418.)

35. Connections between the work of Odoevsky and Tolstoy were recognized by Simon Karlinsky in "A Hollow Shape: The Philosophical Tales of Prince Vladimir Odoevsky," pp. 169–182. Further discussion of these connections can be found in V. I. Sakharov, "Lev Tolstoi i V. F. Odoevskii," pp. 101–115. Most attention in these studies has been paid to connections between "*Zhivoi mertvets*" and "The Death of Ivan Ilich."

36. For a discussion of the possible Fedorov connection to Maiakovsky's work see Edward Brown, pp. 253–256.

37. The scenes in which people try to influence the contents of Podsekal'nikov's suicide note are probably a parody of the section of Dostoevsky's novel *The Possessed* in which Petr Verkhovensky ghostwrites Kirilov's suicide note.

38. Erdman, p. 87.

39. Bulgakov, p. 560.

40. Ibid., p. 558.

41. The words of V. Ia. Vilenkin show the extent to which it was deemed dangerous even to think about Bulgakov's novel in the late '30s. When, after a private reading of excerpts of the novel, Bulgakov asked, "who is Woland?" Vilenkin said that he had guessed but that there was no way he would say. Quoting this statement, Vilenkin adds the following: 'No one could bring himself to give a straight answer. It seemed risky'" (Chudakova, p. 461).

42. Wright, p. 260.

43. Bulgakov, p. 703.

CHAPTER 2

The Seagull as Parody: Symbols and Expectations

WHAT IS THE MEANING OF THE SEAGULL in *The Seagull*? This may seem to be a rather obvious question, but critics considering Anton Chekhov's drama rarely ask it. And when they do, there is no consensus among the responses.[1] This lack of agreement, I will argue, is not coincidental, and is inevitable as long as we continue to pose the question with the expectation that there could be a single answer. In fact, the seagull's meaning is not fixed in Chekhov's play; each main character has his or her own understanding that develops in the course of the play, as does the interpretation of the audience or reader. These varying interpretations are, or at least should be, underpinned by a complex intertwining of subtextual literary references that have never been elucidated, despite the fact that *The Seagull* is almost universally deemed to be "about art."[2]

Let us start our analysis from the beginning of the play. Even before the audience arrives in the theater or the reader takes up the text, they know that they are going to be attending or reading a play entitled *The Seagull*. They begin, therefore, with an expectation that "the seagull" will turn out to be meaningful, like the proverbial gun hanging on the wall in the first act. As a result, for them *The Seagull* becomes a play with a built-in riddle, and part of their job as audience member or reader is to figure out what the eponymous character signifies. The characters, on the other hand, are unaware that they are in a play called *The Seagull*, for no life, even the most theatrically lived one, comes with a preordained title.[3] By the conventions of Chekhovian theater, the characters behave as if they are merely leading their normal lives (abnormal or even histrionic as they may be). In the course of the play a number of characters will indeed come to see that "the seagull" has become a meaningful image, but they make that discovery as part of their own life process rather than having had it suggested to them in advance.

By the end of the play, as the seagull image has accrued meaning through each of its appearances, the audience and at least some of the characters may come to similar conclusions as to its significance. Ultimately, in fact, it could be said that, in parallel to the play's main theme (which examines the suffering and destruction of a crippled artist—and lover—who is unable to survive because of his traumatic family situation), a secondary and generally unrecognized dramatic goal of *The Seagull* is to make it possible for characters and audience to come to some kind of agreement as to the meaning of the title image. But it should not be forgotten that this agreement is reached from opposite directions, as it were; the audience assumes the significance of the bird from the beginning but does not know precisely what kind of significance it has; the characters do not necessarily presume any significance at the outset—they come to recognize the symbolic meaning of the bird through their own life experience.

Given that the seagull motif changes its meaning for both characters and audience in the course of the play, it would seem prudent to analyze Chekhov's drama diachronically in order to see the entire spectrum of possible meanings inherent in the image. But even before we do this, it is necessary to ask what associations are or should be called up by the play's title in the mind of the audience. First and foremost we note the striking use of the name of a bird as the title; for Chekhov's contemporaries, a connection between this play and Henrik Ibsen's *The Wild Duck* would have been hard to avoid.[4] In many respects, Ibsen's dramatic, almost melodramatic, technique and his blunt critique of hypocrisy could not be further removed from Chekhov's mature dramatic method of "indirect action." Still, the sophisticated audience member, who is well aware that he is in a theater watching a consciously created work of literature unfold, should be on the lookout for possible connections to Ibsen's play. And, as we will have occasion to remark in the course of this analysis, this subtextual association is by no means spurious; suffice it to note at this point the link between the bird, the "child" character, and suicide.

The fact that only the audience is, at this point in the play, capable of making subtextual connections to other works points out an aspect of intertextuality that is unique to drama. In lyric poetry, which has received the lion's share of attention from theorists of intertextuality, subtexts are present entirely for the reader. They draw attention to the literary tradition, placing the poem in specific contexts, and allowing for a deepening of meaning when the subtextual links are activated in the reader's mind.[5] In a dramatic work, however, the presence of actors playing characters who by convention do not realize that they are themselves in a literary work allows for more complex subtextual relationships.[6] On the one hand, apparati like the title of the play or an authorial preface can be used to alert the audience to subtextual complexities about which the characters are completely or partially unaware. Individual characters themselves can and frequently do have very different "life experiences" that lead them to provide "their own" subtexts. These are, of course, orchestrated by the author and are at least in principle available to the audience as well; yet they may be so esoteric and unusual that although they underpin the actions of a character they pass essentially unnoticed by all but the most sophisticated audience member. Of course, in drama there are examples of situations in which both characters and audience are aware of the intertextual allusion simultaneously, as in the use of quotations from *Hamlet* in this very play. But even here, there may be a rift between the *Hamlet* that Konstantin Treplev has in mind and the one that a given audience member conjures up. In any case, this is not the place for a long theoretical consideration on how intertexts function in dramatic works; rather, I note the problem as a way to enter the complex world of *The Seagull*, one in which audience and character assumptions do not necessarily coincide on any level, including the subtextual.

Within the play itself, the seagull does not take very long to arrive. In act 1, the young aspiring actress Nina Zarechnaia compares herself to the bird: "My father and his wife won't let me come here. They say it's very bohemian ... they're afraid I'll become an actress. ... But I'm drawn to this lake, as if I were a seagull."[7] For Nina at this point, the metaphorical comparison is both natural and completely innocuous. Her family estate and that of Konstantin are located on the shores of a lake. As yet, she has no foreknowledge of the seagull's impending meaningfulness. Presumably, gulls fly about overhead. For the audience, however, this first mention is neither innocent nor natural. We know that the seagull will be meaningful, we suspect a connection to *The Wild Duck*, and we immediately guess that Nina's identification with the seagull will be in some way analogous to Hedwig Ekdal's, particularly since her position as the young female lead puts her in a parallel position to Hedwig. Nina's candidacy for early self-inflicted death is thus already planted in the audience's mind.

What is more, the careful audience member will have noted Nina's somewhat unusual last name—Zarechnaia. In Russian, the name signifies "beyond the river," and one frequent mythopoetic use of a river or other body of water is as a symbol of the world beyond.[8] Her family, we find out, lives on the other shore of the lake, and thus she functions symbolically as an inhabitant of the world beyond—that is, as a kind of living corpse.

This further underscores her candidacy for early death. Of course, by the end of the play, it will turn out that Chekhov has created these expectations only to frustrate them later. That is to say, although there will indeed be a subtextual connection with *The Wild Duck*, the connection Nina/Hedwig will not turn out to be correct.

The seagull next makes an appearance early in act 2, this time as a realized metaphor in the fullest sense of the word. Konstantin "enters without a hat, carrying a gun [that very one that needs to go off in the fourth act] and a dead sea gull" (p. 38), which he lays at Nina's feet.

> NINA. What is this all about?
> TREPLEV. I was so vile as to kill this sea gull today.
> I lay it at your feet.
> NINA. What's the matter with you?
> (*She lifts the sea gull and gazes at it.*)
> TREPLEV. (*after a pause*). Soon I'll kill myself in the same way. (p. 38)

This scene gives the audience a lot to digest. First of all, we now have a second character who identifies himself with the bird. That is to say, we have a new candidate for the Hedwig Ekdal role. Treplev is at least as sensitive as Nina is, and, what is more, his family is equally dysfunctional. In promising to commit suicide as a kind of sacrifice to love, he directly lines himself up with Hedwig, although in his case the love is romantic rather than expiatory.

Even more interesting is the question, why does Konstantin kill a seagull? It is, after all, a very unusual quarry, one that even the encyclopedic Sergei Aksakov does not tell the Russian sportsman how to hunt.[9] Perhaps no other birds were immediately available. After all, seagulls have a tendency to fly in flocks and to approach people without fear; they are thus relatively easy to shoot and might have appealed to a novice hunter such as Treplev (there are no indications anywhere in the play that he generally goes in for field sports as, say, there are about Trigorin's love of angling). It could be argued that he kills the seagull precisely because Nina has identified herself with this bird in act 1. If so, the killing can be seen not as a harbinger of Konstantin's promised suicide but rather as a coded act of aggression against Nina. Konstantin's act is equivalent to the murder he might like to commit in revenge for Nina's coldness to him. But, at the same time, Konstantin does mention the possibility of suicide, so the audience must also consider him in the Hedwig role. Whether he himself is aware of Ibsen's play is open to debate. Ibsen was, as we noted above, a reasonably well-known writer in the early 1890s, and his work was discussed with some frequency in the early symbolist press.[10]

Whether or not he knew Ibsen, there is a "literary" explanation as to why Konstantin kills a seagull. Although critics have failed to investigate the artistic pedigree of the bird itself, Nina suggests that this should be done when she responds to Treplev's gesture with the lines: "I can't make you out, you speak in symbols. I suppose this sea gull is also a symbol, but excuse me, I don't understand" (p. 39). In fact these lines are important for a number of reasons, first and foremost because they underscore what we noticed earlier—that Nina's earlier identification with the seagull had indeed been an innocent one. For, unless we wish to credit her with a duplicity that seems unlikely, it appears that she has completely forgotten her self-comparison with the bird.

Her suspicion that the bird is a symbol immediately brings up the question, a symbol of what? One would look in vain in encyclopedias of symbols for entries on seagulls; as far as I can tell Chekhov's play marks this bird's first appearance in the avian literary pantheon. But if we see the seagull in functional terms as a large white bird that flies over water and we keep in mind Konstantin's likely reading material, we will not have much difficulty in figuring out why a seagull. Konstantin, as we have already been told, is in search of new dramatic and literary forms. His play, for example, is a mishmash of the latest Western European decadent/ symbolist works (it is worth recalling that at the time Chekhov wrote the play, there was as yet no Russian symbolist movement worth talking about), particularly the plays of the Belgian Francophone writer Maurice Maeterlinck. So we can guess that Konstantin has been reading fairly widely in contemporary French literature, either in the original or in the translations that were beginning to appear regularly in the toniest Russian journals. He would, undoubtedly, have come across the following poem by Charles Baudelaire entitled "L'albatros."[11]

> Souvent pour s'amuser, les hommes d'équipage
> Prennent des albatros, vastes oiseaux des mers,
> Qui suivent, indolents compagnons de voyage,
> Le navire glissant sur les gouffres amers.

A peine les ont-ils déposés sur les planches,
Que ces rois de l'azur, maldroits et honteux
Laissent piteusement leurs grandes ailes blanches
Comme des avirons trainer à côté d'eux

Ce voyageur ailé, comme il est gauche et veule!
Lui, naguère si beau, qu'il est comique et laid!
L'un agace son bec avec un brûle-guele,
L'autre mime, en boitant, linfirme qui volait!

Le Poëte est semblable au prince de nuées
Qui hante la tempête et se rit de l'archer;
Exilé sur le sol au milieu des huées,
Ses ailes de géant l'empêchent de marcher.[12]

The romantic image of the artist in the bathetic last stanza fits perfectly with what we know of Konstantin's self image. Like Baudelaire's poet, Treplev sees himself as misunderstood by the boorish crowd amongst whom he can barely breath, much less walk. The connection between Konstantin and Baudelaire's albatross is made more emphatic by the rather strange second line of the last stanza. The bowman who appears unexpectedly here implies a hunter, of course, and encourages Konstantin to see himself as both hunter and hunted simultaneously, thereby strengthening for the audience the potential suicide subtext via the wild duck, which, it will be remembered, appeared in the Ekdal family after having been winged by Werle on a hunting trip. Furthermore, although neither of the Russian translations that Konstantin would have had available pick up on this, the unexpectedly appearing archer implies a connection to Hamlet, who in his most famous soliloquy rails against "slings and arrows."[13] And by this point in the play the audience is already aware of Treplev's Hamlet complex.

The series of subtextual references occasioned by the metaphorical and actual appearance of the seagull is, at this point, augmented by the commentary of the last major character in the play who will be linked to the bird—Trigorin. Having seen the dead bird lying on the ground, he asks Nina, "and what's this?" (p. 43). The following dialogue ensues:

NINA. A sea gull. Konstantin killed it.
TRIGORIN. A beautiful bird. I really don't feel like leaving.

Try and talk Irina into staying. (*Writes in his notebook.*)
NINA. What are you writing?
TRIGORIN. Oh, just taking notes.... A subject flashed through
my head.... (*Puts the notebook away.*) A subject for a short story:
A young girl lives all her life on the shore of a lake. She loves the
lake and is happy and free, like a sea gull. By chance a man comes,
sees her, and having nothing better to do, destroys her. Here, like
this sea gull. (*Pause.*)

Two important things happen here. The first is that Trigorin, like the
other two major characters, self-identifies with the seagull, albeit in a more
oblique manner than either of the others. It has already been noted for us
that seagulls are particularly attracted to the lake (Nina said so in act 1),
and so Trigorin's desire not to leave puts him in the seagull category.
This connection is strengthened by his decision to write a story employing
the seagull metaphor, thus inscribing his own work into this symbolic
paradigm and incorporating it into a new creative context simultaneously.
The second thing is that by placing the girl in the seagull role in his
proposed story, Trigorin encourages the audience to switch back to the
expectation that Nina will be the play's tragic victim and, perhaps, he
recalls to Nina the fact that she had indeed identified herself with the
bird some days earlier. Who is to be placed in the role of the destroyer,
however, is less clear. For although it is Konstantin who actually killed the
bird, and at this point in the play the audience would be justified in seeing
him as the likely source of evil in Nina's life, upcoming events will indicate
that Trigorin has by this point already imagined himself in this role. Rather
than behaving as a proper realist writer (which is what the somewhat
old-fashioned Trigorin appears to be)—that is, observing life and then
incorporating it into a work of art—Trigorin here engages in a bit of what
the symbolists would call life-creation (*zhiznetvorchestvo*).[14] He creates
a story that he then feels compelled to live out.

By this point in the play, the audience's expectations are maximally
confused. The belief that the seagull will become a meaningful image in
the play, as suggested by the title, has been amply confirmed. But the
meaning of the image, as well as whom to identify with the bird and at
what level of metaphorical connection, is completely unclear. Three
separate characters could potentially play the role of the seagull—one
which, at this point, appears to be that of the sacrificial victim à la Hedvig

Ekdal, although literary subtexts engage other potential levels of meaning in the image. But two of these characters appear also to be vying for the role of the seagull's destroyer.

It is precisely at this moment in the play that Chekhov tricks his audience. On the one hand, at the beginning of act 3, which takes place a week after the action of act 2, he has Trigorin and Nina recall the portentous image.

> NINA. Think of me now and then.
> TRIGORIN. I will. I will think of you on that sunny day—
> remember?—a week ago . . . you were wearing a white dress . . .
> we spoke . . . there was a white sea gull on the beach.
> NINA (*pensively*). Yes, a sea gull . . . (p. 45)

The connection of the white dress with the white bird clearly reinforces the idea of Nina as the metaphorical bird, and her pensive reply indicates that she has, by now, come to believe that her life could be a play properly entitled *The Seagull*. All of this encourages the audience to feel a (false) sense of security regarding their understanding of the play's central image.

At the same time, Chekhov has done something here that he rarely does in his major dramas. He has intentionally left out what will turn out to be a crucial event. That is, he neglects to let us know that Trigorin, ever the literalist, chose not merely to immortalize the bird as a metaphorical image in one of his stories, but also that he asked Shamraev to have the actual object taken to a taxidermist's and stuffed. We will see just how significant this omission is for destabilizing audience expectations about the nature of the seagull when the bird reappears in act 4. For now, however, the seagull, real or metaphorical, proceeds to disappear completely from the play for the rest of this act and for part of the final one.

When the seagull does reappear in act 4 it first does so metaphorically. In his description of Nina's life during the two years that have passed between acts 3 and 4, Treplev tells Dorn that "her mind was a bit unhinged. She signed her letters 'Sea Gull.' In Pushkin's 'The Water-Nymph' ["Rusalka"] the miller says he's a raven [in Russian "voron"], and she kept insisting she's a sea gull" (p. 60). At the beginning of the play Nina forgot she had compared herself with a seagull, thereby rendering Konstantin's shooting the bird an exercise in one-way communication. In symmetrical response, as it were, Konstantin has apparently forgotten about shooting the bird—and therefore Nina's attempt at symbolic communication with him through the seagull metaphor is equally ineffective. In both cases, however, communication with the audience succeeds, and they, having recalled both these instances as well as Trigorin's proposed story about the seagull, think that they have now finally figured out the mystery set by the play's title: Nina is the seagull/victim/Hedwig; Trigorin is the evil male figure; and Konstantin's shooting of the bird appears to have been a red herring designed to complicate the story.

It is quite curious that Konstantin should bring up Pushkin's "Rusalka" at this point, and even more curious that he should mention the obscure miller.[15] If, however, we turn our attention not to the work or the character but rather to the specific bird mentioned we may understand the logic of the reference. For the bird with which the miller identifies is the same one that would later be memorialized by Edgar Allen Poe in a work that every Russian aspiring decadent knew by heart.[16] In that poem, the poet sits in his study hoping that, although he has lost his beloved Lenore in this world, he will yet be reunited with her in the next. The fiendish raven dashes these hopes in the following stanza:

Prophet! said I, "thing of evil! – prophet still, if bird or devil!
By that Heaven that bends above us – by that God we both adore –
Tell this soul with sorrow laden if, within the distant Aidenn,
It shall clasp a sainted maiden whom the angels name Lenore –
Clasp a rare and radiant maiden whom the angels name Lenore."
Quoth the Raven "Nevermore."[17]

Insofar as Konstantin has conscious or unconscious hopes of winning Nina back, the bird subtext implies that they will be in vain. What is more, the ultimate stanza of Poe's poem hints that Konstantin will himself never be able to escape from under the sign of the bird:

And the Raven, never flitting, *still* is sitting, still is sitting
On the pallid bust of Pallas just above my chamber door;
And his eyes have all the seeming of a demon's that is dreaming,
And the lamp-light o'er him streaming throws his shadow on the floor;
And my soul from out that shadow that lies floating on the floor
Shall be lifted – nevermore!

All in all, this passage serves to indicate that Konstantin has not really forgotten his ill-advised hunting escapade but has only suppressed its memory.

And indeed, our sense of equilibrium is not destined to last very long, for only moments later the seagull reappears, this time, potentially at least, in corporeal form. Shamraev says to Trigorin: "Boris Alexeevich, we still have that thing of yours." To Trigorin's amazed "What thing?" Shamraev responds, "Konstantin Gavrilovich once shot a sea gull, and you told me to have it stuffed." Trigorin now becomes the third character to forget all about the bird.[18] This consistent pattern whereby characters in the play mention the seagull apparently for some symbolic purpose and then proceed to forget all about it would be eminently comic were it not for the fact that each time this happens the seagull is picked up by a different member of the trio as if it were a relay baton. In this case it is Konstantin, who, having heard Shamraev's account of how the seagull came to be preserved, evidently begins to recover his suppressed memories relating to the long-past event. For after hearing Shamraev's little speech and Trigorin's uncomprehending reply he says, "How dark it is! I don't know why I feel so uneasy" (p. 64).

This vague uneasiness may not only be caused by his inchoate recollections of his earlier action. It may also derive from a recognition that he had been wrong to associate the seagull with the albatross of Baudelaire's poem. Rather, its appearance in the flesh likely recalls to him an earlier and much more ominous poetic incarnation of the albatross—Samuel Taylor Coleridge's "The Rime of the Ancient Mariner," a text he would have done well to have had in mind when he first killed the bird.[19] As opposed to the Baudelaire poem, in which the albatross is captured and mocked but survives, in "The Rime," Coleridge's sailor, like Konstantin, is so vile as actually to kill the innocent creature. "'God save thee, ancient Mariner! / From the fiends, that plague thee thus!—/ Why look'st thou so?'—With my crossbow / I shot the ALBATROSS."[20] Although Konstantin had managed, it might have appeared, to forget all about the seagull incident (to the point of being unable to recollect why Nina would have signed her letters "Sea Gull") he now begins to suspect that he has never escaped from under the sign of the dead bird. He fears that, like the ancient mariner, he will be forced to wear the albatross around his neck forever.[21] This is why it is significant that the bird has been stuffed. For it is precisely its physical presence that brings to mind the consequences of the ancient mariner's actions.

The ominous image of the seagull/albatross is developed further in Konstantin by the appearance of Nina herself a moment later, and her famous speech in which she describes her life since leaving her family estate to go on the stage. In the first part of this speech she says: "I'm a sea gull. . . . No, that's not it." This line is particularly significant because it indicates that for her, as for Konstantin, the seagull/albatross has been hanging around on the edge of her consciousness ever since those fateful days, although in her case the recognition of the seagull's power is far more overt. What is more, in these lines she specifically refuses to identify herself with the seagull. Considering that we know she formerly signed her letters "Sea Gull," this marks a major change, and it leads us (along with Konstantin) to wonder with whom the seagull is to be identified if not with her.

In her second recollection of the bird she also notes the other two possible seagull figures in the play, saying: "I'm a sea gull. No, that's not right. . . . Remember—you shot a sea gull? By chance a man came, saw a sea gull, and having nothing better to do destroyed it. . . . A subject for a short story. . . . No, that's not right" (p. 67). The placement of the repeated "that's not right" here is crucial. The first one seconds her renunciation of her own candidacy, and the second rejects Trigorin in the role. That leaves Konstantin as the only seagull. Now a second literary subtext, and an equally ominous one, comes into play both for Konstantin and the audience. As the character identified with the bird as well as with the bird's killer, Konstantin may now recognize his kinship with Hedwig Ekdal (who was supposed to shoot the bird but killed herself instead). Finally, at the end of her speech Nina leaves, dashing any remaining hopes on Konstantin's part that they will be united in this life. In so doing she activates the final important literary subtext, that of Poe's "Raven."

Konstantin's suicide at the play's end now becomes perfectly comprehensible. It is the ominous conjunction of three literary subtexts connected to the seagull image that does him in. "The Raven" tells him that Nina is lost forever; "The Ancient Mariner" tells him that the loss was his own fault and that it will haunt him forever; and *The Wild Duck* suggests the possibility of expiatory self-sacrifice. He who lives by the bird, dies by the bird. In the final analysis, then, Konstantin kills himself because of his belief in symbols, whose meaning he understands quite literally.[22] His life drama, it turns out, could well be called *The Seagull*, and it is written by him just as badly as his ill-fated symbolist play. He rings down the curtain on the former as abruptly as he had on the latter.

But what makes *The Seagull* a great play is that by the end it is only Konstantin who thinks this way about the seagull. That is, the bird is a highly multivalent symbol in Chekhov's play. Nina, unlike the erudite Konstantin, is almost certainly blithely unaware of the literary subtexts underlying the image. She initially used it completely accidentally, as we recall, and it has followed her around ever since. Nevertheless, the fact that in her last speech she renounces her connection to the bird is significant. For her, the seagull is indeed a symbol of lost youth and innocence, but it is a symbol that she is now ready to get beyond. Insofar as her life was once a drama called *The Seagull*, the curtain has gone down and she is ready for her next role. Trigorin has simply forgotten all about the seagull in any of its manifestations. For him, by the end of the play, the image has come to signify nothing but itself: a meaningless dead stuffed bird.

But what of the audience? We began the play with the expectation that the seagull would be a highly meaningful image, something very much like the duck in Ibsen's play. Quite clearly, these anticipations have been dashed. The seagull is indeed meaningful, but unlike the wild duck it does not contain a definable core meaning; rather, its meaning shifts from character to character and from act to act. Chekhov's audience learns two important things. The first is that because a symbol is multivalent, the imputation to it of a single meaning leads inevitably to the flattening out of that meaning. The second is just how dangerous it is to live your life in the forest of symbols. On the surface, the former brings Chekhov's play close to Ibsen's. In speaking of *The Wild Duck* Maurice Vallency notes:

> As a metaphor, the wounded bird serves to characterize the lives and souls of almost all the characters in the play from Old Ekdal to Gregers Werle; it refers to Hedwig in still another way; and it is used emblematically to describe in general the therapeutic role of illusion in life. In the end the Wild Duck serves to unify in a single figure the entire action of the play: so much meaning radiates from this symbol that anything that serves to define it, serves also to restrict its efficacy. From Chekhov's *The Seagull* to Graham Greene's *The Living Room*, no device has been found more useful in searching out the poetic core of a dramatic action than a metaphor of this sort.[23]

The seagull in Chekhov's play is an even more complex symbol, however, because it is manipulated in a much more conscious fashion by the characters in the play and because of its subtextual substrate. And yet, in the end, Chekhov uses the seagull not just more complexly but quite differently from Ibsen. For while in Ibsen the wild duck leads to symbolic overload as each character ends up being identified with it, *The Seagull* follows exactly the reverse pattern. Characters do identify themselves with the seagull in the course of the play, but they eventually refuse this identification. That is, they all do except Treplev, who is left standing in this game of dramatic musical chairs. And, in the end, identification with the symbol turns out to be dangerous, for it is the direct cause of his death.

Why should Chekhov have written a highly symbolic drama about the dangers of a belief in symbolism? To answer this question we must note one extremely important fact about Russian culture at the turn of the twentieth century. From our (frequently overly teleological) point of view, Russian realism appears to have hit a dead end in the early 1880s, following the death of Dostoevsky in 1881, the death of Turgenev in 1883, and Tolstoy's general renunciation of his earlier artistic work at about the same time. In its stead, so the literary histories tell us, came Symbolism, as practiced by a first generation (sometimes called Decadents) consisting of Dmitrii Merezhkovsky, Valerii Briusov, Konstantin Bal'mont, and a second-generation led by Andrei Bely, Viacheslav Ivanov, and Aleksandr Blok. These successive waves of symbolists were, we are told, the harbingers of all the profusion of modernist Russian cultural movements of the early twentieth century.[24] What teleological histories overlook, however, is that the triumph of symbolism was by no means guaranteed. The putative symbolists had to compete not with nonentities, but with major writers such as Ivan Bunin, Anton Chekhov, and Maksim Gorky. Thus, in the middle of the 1890s a complex battle for literary supremacy was being fought in Russia, and it is within this context that Chekhov's antisymbolist symbolic play needs to be understood.

It should be recalled that the first efforts of the fledgling Russian symbolists to break into print were almost laughable. In 1894 Valerii Briusov and Aleksandr Lang published, at their own expense, a series of volumes entitled *Russian Symbolists*. As Joan Grossman puts it: "Briusov later maintained that the purpose of these volumes was to provide models of various poetic forms. Moreover, by asserting that there was a Russian

Symbolist school, he hoped to create one and ultimately to win acceptance for the new poetry. The reception given the first issue made clear, however, that neither result would soon be forthcoming."[25] Indeed, it would be at least five more years before Russian symbolist poets would produce significant quantities of successful work.

Yet, paradoxically enough, before there were successful Russian symbolists, three devastating parodies of symbolism by Russian authors had appeared. They were to be found in Tolstoy's *What Is Art?* (1896), in Vladimir Solov'ev's article *"Eshche o simvolistakh"* ("One More Time About the Symbolists," 1895), and in Chekhov's *The Seagull* (1896). The first of these directly savaged French symbolism, with only fleeting reference to a Russian connection, but the latter two specifically attacked the (barely existing) Russian symbolism. Tolstoy's and Solov'ev's parodies attempt to deflate only the poetic rhetoric of the symbolist movement, while Chekhov's is the most thoroughgoing, attacking both symbolist writing practices and, as we have seen, the entire life-creation aspect of symbolism.

Of the three, Tolstoy's is not a parody in the strictest sense, for he does not actually write anything "in the style of"; rather he elaborates a method he had first used in *War and Peace*. He quotes extensively from those with whom he disagrees, providing, for his part, a savage running commentary. Nevertheless, the effect is one of parody, and a nasty one at that, lacking as it does the slightest shred of sympathy for the strivings of the writers in question. After quoting in full verses by Baudelaire, Verlaine, Mallarmé, and Maeterlinck, Tolstoy ends his consideration of literary symbolism by saying: "I beg the reader to be at the pains of reading through the samples I cite in Appendix II of the celebrated and esteemed young poets—Griffin, Verhaeren, Moréas, and Montesquiou. It is important to do so in order to form a clear conception of the present position of art, and not to suppose, as many do, that Decadentism is an accidental or transitory phenomenon." He then adds, with a stroke of comic genius, "To avoid the reproach of having selected the worst verses, I have copied out of each volume the poem which happened to stand on page 28."[26]

Given Tolstoy's well-publicized dislike of difficult works of art lacking a religious impulse and written by and for elites, his disdain for the latest in decadent literature probably surprised no one. And in any case, although he mentions the existence of Russian symbolists in his general assault, he does not even find their literary efforts worthy of attack. The parodic criticism of Vladimir Solov'ev, however, was of another order. In the first place, he himself had written a certain number of protosymbolist verses. And, in the second, a few years later his philosophical ideas would provide the basic ideological underpinnings for the so-called second generation of Russian symbolists. In fact, Solov'ev's three reviews of the short books produced by Valerii Briusov and his friends are suffused with a certain sympathy for the fledgling movement, but his witty comments and the three parodic poems he appended to his last review are, if anything, more devastating than Tolstoy's invective. In his review of the first volume, he criticized the young symbolists for excessive copying of European models, for a lack of clarity, and for vulgarity. He continued and deepened these criticisms in the second review, but he saved his most effective and amusing critical salvos for what turned out to be his final review on the subject. Responding to Briusov's charge that he had distorted the meaning of the symbolists' verse, replied: "I could not have distorted the meaning of these poems—because they lack any meaning whatsoever." He follows this with a number of solecisms culled from the latest collection, and then concludes his discussion of original Russian symbolist poetry as follows: "I must note that one poem in this collection possesses a clear and certain meaning. It is very short, – exactly one line: 'Oh, cover your pale legs.' For crystal clarity, of course, 'otherwise you'll catch cold' should have been added, but even without this, Briusov's words of advice, evidently directed to a person suffering from anemia, make up the most sensible work of all of symbolist literature, not merely Russian but foreign as well."[27]

The grand finale to Solov'ev's review consists of three poems written "in symbolist style" that mercilessly parody the favorite tricks of the young Briusov. The poems are filled with unlikely and extravagant metaphors, oxymoronic imagery, unconvincing neologisms, and unmotivated repetitions. They are also noticeably lacking any intellectual and philosophical depth. Ultimately, what the reviews and parodies illustrate is not that Solov'ev was opposed to symbolism, but rather that he was disappointed by those aspects of symbolism that Briusov and his friends adopted. Instead of attempting a serious artistic synthesis of the real and the ideal, Briusov's version of symbolism merely borrowed the most obvious surface devices of his French predecessors. That is, Solov'ev criticized the early Russian symbolists for not being symbolist enough. His disappointment lay in that fact that they borrowed the outer form of symbolism "to express vulgarity, obscenity, and stupidity."[28] In general, however, Solov'ev stuck to specific literary infelicities in his dissection of Briusov's work, only occasionally noting that were the symbolists to act in the manner of their lyrical personas, trouble would result.

Like Tolstoy and Solov'ev, Chekhov was interested in attacking the literary practice of the nascent decadents/symbolists. Although we have not given it any serious consideration in this essay, Konstantin's play is unquestionably a parody, "a concoction of melodramatic posturing and mannered symbolism," as Robert Louis Jackson has put it succinctly.[29] What has generally been overlooked, however, is that Chekhov's parody extends well beyond the literary to encompass the psychology and the mode of being adopted by the early Russian symbolists. And, what is more, Chekhov does not merely attack. In his use of the seagull, Chekhov proposes a completely different but no less symbolic art. His symbolism is not based on a mystical connection of the phenomenal and noumenal worlds; rather it grows organically out of nineteenth-century Russian realism, taking as its starting point the recognition that material objects take on symbolic meaning because individuals invest them with their own meanings. Moreover he recognizes that because no two individuals have the same experience of the world, a symbol is a polyvalent and always shifting placeholder for the content of an individual's fantasies, dreams, and memories.

Let us return for a moment to Chekhov's portrayal of decadent attitudes to life. Ivan Goncharov had once claimed: "It is difficult, . . . and in my opinion simply impossible, to portray a life that has not yet taken form, where its forms have not settled and characters have not been stratified into types."[30] But what is almost amazing about the portrait of Treplev is that despite the fact that the Russian decadent type had by no means been formed when Chekhov wrote his play, he captures its basic outline to uncanny perfection. Indeed, it sometimes seems as if Chekhov must have had access to the most private diaries of the as-yet-unknown decadents. Compare, for example, Treplev's self-view with that expressed by Briusov in a diary entry for March 4, 1894: "Talent, even genius, by honest means earns only gradual success, if that. That's not enough! For me it's not enough. I must choose another way. . . . And I see it: Decadence. Yes! Whatever one may say, whether it is false, or ridiculous, it is moving ahead, developing, and the future belongs to it, especially when it finds a worthy leader. And that leader will be I! Yes, I."[31] In general, Chekhov's hostility to Treplev's way of being is directly connected to the symbolist desire to fuse life and art. Such an attempt must have struck him as nothing more than the latest irresponsible phase of the Russian intelligentsia, a group he had once described with a series of adjectives that could easily be applied to Treplev: "hypocritical, dishonest, hysterical, ill-bred and lazy."[32] Chekhov's ability to capture the nuances of decadent behavior extends all the way to the end of the play. Treplev's suicide, as we have already seen, was motivated by his tendency to read his life as if it were an artistic text. But the fascination with suicide in general became a well-elaborated part of Russian modernist life-creation practice. Treplev's literary suicide, then, can be seen as the harbinger in a line that came to include such real-life figures as Vsevolod Kniazev (who posthumously became a protagonist in Anna Akhmatova's *Poem Without a Hero*), Sergei Esenin, Vladimir Maiakovsky, and Marina Tsvetaeva.

Ultimately, however, like Solov'ev, Chekhov attacks symbolism in its early Russian variant not merely to discredit it, but also to propose a completely different version of symbolism in its place. For Chekhov, by this point in his career, had left the confines of Russian realism far behind and was well on his way to creating what might be called a fully realistic symbolism. The basis of Chekhov's symbolism was the realization that an object that takes on symbolic value does so as a result of the specific meanings attached to it over time by particular individuals. An object, like a word, only has meaning in the context of its usage, so it is as futile to expect that the symbol could have a specific ideal meaning as it is to think that its real essence could be agreed upon by any two individuals. In *The Seagull* each character creates and recreates his or her own symbolic meaning for the bird. It is left to the audience to decide not which is the "correct" meaning, but rather to see how these various meanings interact to create drama, both staged and human. Exactly the same thing, by the way, could be said about the cherry orchard in Chekhov's final play, or about Moscow in *The Three Sisters*. In every case, what counts are expectations, those of characters and those of the audience. The drama lies in their symbolic interplay.

NOTES

1. In her article "Chekhov's *Seagull*: Ethereal Creature or Stuffed Bird?" Ellen Chances summarizes a number of interpretations belonging to what she calls the "ethereal bird school." She tells us that Leonid Grossman and David Magarshak identify the bird primarily with Nina's fate. V. V. Ermilov, on the other hand, connects the seagull to Treplev. Maurice Valency is even more general, equating the seagull with the beauty of all living things. See Debreczeny and Eekman, *Chekhov's Art of Writing: A Collection of Critical Essays*, p. 27. Chances herself attempts to found a "stuffed bird" school of interpretation that brings out the ironic potential in the seagull. Eli Rozik has proposed a complex reading of the seagull image to prove that the play is best read within the confines of naturalism. The seagull, for Rozik, is not a symbol at all, but a motif that functions to bring out Chekhov's supposed naturalist intent. See his 1988 article "The Interpretative Function of the 'Seagull' Motif in *The Seagull*."

2. This is not to say that the intertextual dimension to Chekhov's play has been entirely ignored. Critics have paid ample attention to the relationship between Chekhov's play and artistic texts directly mentioned in it, particularly *Hamlet* and Guy de Maupassant's sketch "*Sur l'eau.*" For a consideration of the former see Thomas G. Winner, "Chekhov's *Seagull* and Shakespeare's *Hamlet*: A Study of a Dramatic Device," *American Slavic and East European Review* 15 (February 1956): pp. 103–111. For the relationship between Chekhov and Maupassant see Ellen Chances's article cited in the previous note, as well as Jerome H. Katsell, "Chekhov's *The Seagull* and Maupassant's *Sur l'eau*" in *Chekhov's Great Plays. A Critical Anthology*, edited by Jean-Pierre Barricelli (New York: New York University Press, 1981), pp. 18–34. But the intertextual nature of the seagull itself has been almost entirely overlooked.

3. To be sure, like many of Chekhov's characters, those in *The Seagull* frequently behave as if they were in a play, but they still do not know its title. For more a detailed discussion of the theatrical impulse in Chekhov's characters, see Morson, 1990–91.

4. Ibsen's play was published in November 1884, and had already been widely staged in Scandinavia by the next year. In 1891 it received triumphant productions in France and in Germany. The first Russian translation appeared in 1892, but the play was known to educated Russians even before this. Thus, Tolstoy's diary for August 20, 1890, notes that he had read the play, which he disliked. (See Martin Nag, *Ibsen i russisk andsliv* [Oslo: Gyldendal Norsk Forlag A/S, 1967], p. 99). According to Nils Ake Nilsson, the period 1891–92 marked a surge in interest in Scandinavian drama in general and Ibsen's work in particular. See his *Ibsen in Russland* (Stockholm: Alquist & Wiksell, 1958), p. 12.

    That the Ibsen connection was indeed obvious to contemporaries can be seen in the criticism Chekhov's play received after its first reading by the Theatrical-literary Committee whose approval was necessary if the play was to be staged. They reported that the play "suffers from serious flaws. The 'symbolism,' or more accurately 'Ibsenism' (in this case even too close, if one recalls Ibsen's *Wild Duck*) that goes through the whole play like a red thread is truly unpleasant." Quoted in the notes to Chekhov, 1974–1983, 6:505.

5. For important work on subtexts and their function in Russian literature, see Renate Lachmann, *Memory and Literature: Intertextuality in Russian Modernism*, Igor Smirnov, *Porozhdenie interteksta* (Saint Petersburg, 1995), and Ekaterina Kozitskaia, *Smysloobrazuiushchaia funktsiia tsitaty v poeticheskom tekste* (Tver, 1998).

6. To some extent, the same thing can be said about novels, but the existence of actors playing the characters in a play encourages us to see them as more independent of the author than are characters in a novel, and therefore allows for more finely tuned intertextual play between their expectations and ours.

7. Anton Chekhov, *The Seagull*, in Ehre, 1992, p. 23. Further quotations from *The Seagull* will be made in the text of this chapter by reference to page numbers of this edition.

8. For a detailed discussion of the mythopoetic symbolism of bodies of water, see Boris Gasparov, "Poetika 'Slovo o polku Igoreve'," *Wiener Slawistischer Almanach* Sonderband 12 (1984): pp. 129–138.

9. Aksakov lists at least fourteen water birds worthy of being shot (most of them wild ducks, by the way), in his encyclopedic *Zapiski ruzheinogo okhotnika* (*Notes of a Provincial Wildfowler*) without mentioning any member of the gull family.

10. For a survey of the literary material that would have made up the reading list of a young writer in Treplev's position, see Georgette Donchin, *The Influence of French Symbolism on Russian Poetry*, pp. 32–75.

11. Baudelaire's poem had been translated into Russian twice by the time Chekhov wrote *The Seagull*. Dmitrii Merezhkovsky's translation appeared in his volume *Stikhotvoreniia* in 1888, and Petr Iakubovich published his in the journal *Severnyi vestnik* in 1890. For more on this and in general on the importance of Baudelaire for Russian writers of Konstantin's stripe, see Adrian Wanner, *Baudelaire in Russia* (Gainesville: University Press of Florida, 1996).

12. In James McGowan's English translation the poem reads as follows:

> Often, when bored, the sailors of the crew
> Trap albatross, the great birds of the seas,
> Mild travelers escorting in the blue
> Ships gliding on the ocean's mysteries.
>
> And when they have deposed them on the planks,
> Hurt and distraught, these kings of all outdoors
> Piteously let trail along their flanks
> Their great white wings, dragging like useless oars.
>
> This voyager, how comical and weak!
> Once handsome, how unseemly and inept!
> One sailor pokes a pipe into his beak,
> Another mocks the flier's hobbled step.
>
> The Poet is a kinsman in the clouds
> Who laughs at archers, loves a stormy day;
> But on the ground, among the hooting crowds,
> He cannot walk, his wings are in the way.

From *66 Translations from Charles Baudelaire's Les Fleurs du Mal* (Peoria, IL: Spoon River Poetry Press, 1985), p. 7.

13. That the Shakespeare allusion is not entirely far-fetched can be seen from the translation produced by George Dillon in 1936. He renders the final stanza as: "The Poet is like that wild inheritor of the cloud, / A rider of storms, above the range of arrows and slings; / Exiled on earth, at bay amid the jeering crowd, / He cannot walk for his unmanageable wings." *Flowers of Evil* (New York: Harper & Brothers, 1936), p. 147.
14. For a series of insightful essays on life-creation, see Paperno and Grossman, *Creating Life*.
15. The reference is not quite as obscure as it would seem, however, because although Pushkin's play was rarely performed in the second half of the nineteenth century, the mad miller's soliloquy, in its operatic form as composed by Dargomyzhsky, was an absolute chestnut in concert performance in this period.
16. Bal'mont's famous translation of this poem appeared in 1895.
17. Poe, p. 756.
18. It is an interesting directorial question as to whether Shamraev should actually produce the bird at this point. Nothing in the stage directions says that he should, but from here to the end of the play the bird's shadow unquestionably hangs over everything. I am inclined to think that the bird should make an appearance at this point, in stuffed form, to indicate its centrality to the play as a whole.
19. As opposed to Baudelaire and Poe, Coleridge was not wildly popular among the early symbolists. Nevertheless, "The Rime of the Ancient Mariner" would have been readily available to Konstantin in Russian translation. The work was first translated into Russian as "Skazanie o Starom Morekhode" in 1851 by F. Miller. This translation was republished in 1875 in N. V. Gerbel's popular anthology entitled *Angliiskie poety v biografiiakh i obraztsakh*. In 1878 the poem was retranslated by N. Pushkarev, and it was translated again by the proto-symbolist Apollon Korinfsky in 1893. For two Russian translations as well as an informative article on Coleridge in Russia, see A. A. Elistravova and A. N. Gorbunov, eds., *S. T. Koleridzh, Stikhi* (Moscow, 1974).
20. Samuel Taylor Coleridge, "The Rime of the Ancient Mariner" 2.78–2.82.
21. The missing link between Baudelaire's relatively innocent albatross and the more sinister one of Coleridge might have been provided by Melville's *Moby-Dick*. In the chapter entitled "The Whiteness of the Whale," Melville provides a long disquisition on the ominous character of various white objects, among them the albatross. And in a long footnote to that chapter he appends a description of the first albatross he ever saw, which had been captured and was being tortured by sailors much as Baudelaire describes in his poem. See Herman Melville, *Moby-Dick or The Whale* (Evanston, IL: Northwestern University Press, 1988), pp. 188–195.
22. *In Narrative and Freedom: The Shadows of Time*, Gary Saul Morson makes a similar assertion regarding Anna Karenina's suicide. See the sections on pp. 71–79.
23. As quoted in the Norton Critical Edition of *The Wild Duck*, edited by Dounia B. Christiani (New York: W.W. Norton & Company, 1968), p. 207.
24. Typical of this teleological approach are the following comments: "The 1880s in Russian literature were a transitional decade separating two literary eras.... It was the 1890s which became the decade of rebellion, and heralded a new 'golden age' in Russian poetry. In the early years of the decade the general features of the new literary trend become apparent. They express a yearning for artistic and individual freedom, a protest against the civic poetry which predominated in Russia in the

second half of the nineteenth century. At the same time, they reflect the ferment of the intellectual life of the period, the contemporary 'schism of the soul.' A new kind of poetry was needed to express the new mood" (Donchin, *The Influence of French Symbolism on Russian Poetry*, p. 8).

25. Grossman, pp. 36–37.
26. Tolstoy, *What Is Art?*, pp. 89–90.
27. Solov'ev, pp. 152–153.
28. Kushlina, pp. 35–36.
29. Jackson, p. 3.
30. Quoted in Ehre, 1973, p. 74.
31. Quoted in Grossman, p. 35.
32. From a letter to Ivan Orlov of 22 February 1899. Quoted in Chekhov, *Letters*, p. 341.

CHAPTER 3

Intertextual and Sexual Desire in
Aleksandr Blok's *The Unknown Woman*

THE UNKNOWN WOMAN (*Neznakomka*—also sometimes translated as "The Stranger"), the title of Aleksandr Blok's 1906 lyric drama, immediately offers itself to us as a mystery. Who is this unknown woman? And will we come to know her in the course of the drama? For anyone acquainted with Russian literature and culture in general, and with the work of Blok in particular, the title suggests a second, intertextual mystery. First, what is the relationship between the play and the author's celebrated lyric, also entitled "The Unknown Woman"?[1] And, furthermore, what is the relationship between this unknown woman and other figures who either are or could be referred to by the same mysterious title in the Russian literary and cultural tradition? The latter question is especially interesting because Blok took the unusual step of providing his drama with two epigraphs drawn from Fedor Dostoevsky's novel *The Idiot*, both of which describe the figure of Nastasia Filippovna. Thus, as opposed to the plays considered in previous chapters, Blok's drama wears its intertextual connections (at least some of them) on its sleeve.

But before turning to a discussion of intertextuality in relation to the play, it is necessary to recall its plot, particularly as the work is not well known either to Russian or American readers.[2] I borrow here the excellent synopsis provided by Timothy Westphalen:

> It is divided into "visions" rather than acts, and the first opens in a bar. On the wallpaper "exactly identical ships" . . . cut through "blue waters." At the counter stand the Owner and his brother, who look exactly alike except for their mustaches . . . Snippets of conversation can be heard. Two men argue about how much one of them paid for his hat, while a third man tries to reconcile them. Another man rises from his seat and makes his way unsteadily to a tub of crayfish. . . . The scene then shifts to another conversation, this one involving a Seminarian, who goes on at length about a woman who danced so wonderfully he "could have kissed her, I tell you, right on the lips." His boon companions tease him about his infatuation, calling him a

dreamer. At a nearby window sits "the spitting image of Verlaine," who mumbles over and over to himself...Nearby, at a second window, sits "the spitting image of Hauptmann." A young man runs in and informs him that a woman is waiting for him. Hauptmann, however. does not get too excited, instead, he tells the young man to let her wait. Verlaine again mumbles loudly to himself, and finally one of the main characters, the Poet, makes his entrance. He tells the Owner how he wandered the streets, seeing the eyes of hundreds of women. Then he came upon the "beautiful face of the Stranger." At this point, Verlaine begins mumbling yet again, the Seminarian waxes rhapsodic about his dancer, and Hauptmann tells the Young Man to let the woman wait a little while longer. A man in a coat enters, trying to sell a cameo that depicts the Woman who Rules the World. The Poet is enchanted and buys it. . . . In turn, the Poet and then the Seminarian go into raptures, the first over the cameo, the second over his dancer. . . . The first "vision" comes to an end with Verlaine once more mumbling to himself, Hauptmann telling the Young Man to let the woman wait, the Girl bidding her escort farewell, the Seminarian praising his dancer, and the Poet conjuring the Stranger to appear. As the action of the "vision" ends, the whole bar seems to be diving somewhere: the walls part and the ceiling opens up to reveal a cold and blue winter sky.

As the second vision begins, the bar has disappeared, and in its place the audience finds "the end of a street at the edge of the city." A dark, deserted bridge spans a large river, and ships can be seen on either side. Beyond the bridge, an avenue lined with streetlights stretches out seemingly endlessly. On the bridge is an Astronomer who marvels at the infinity of stars above him. He disdainfully watches as doormen throw the drunken Poet in the snow. The Astronomer again looks up and sees a falling star. The star falls to earth, and a moment later the Stranger walks onto the bridge. She is met there by the Blue One. They talk, and it becomes apparent that the Stranger seeks earthly passion, while the Blue One can only worship her with an otherworldly love. The Blue One disappears from the bridge, and a Gentleman appears. He offers the Stranger the physical passion she seeks. When they have departed, the Astronomer reappears and mourns the fallen star he has named "Maria." The Poet rejoins him, asking if he has seen the

Stranger. The Astronomer is insulted by what he, in the face of the loss he has just suffered, deems coarseness. To the Poet's sadness, he does confirm seeing a woman with a "blue gentleman." However, the snow has covered their tracks. The second vision ends with the Poet and the Astronomer attempting to prove whose loss is greater. As the action ends, the snow becomes heavier and forms out of the distance white walls that thicken.

These white walls become those of a large drawing room, the setting of the third vision. As it begins the Host greets a guest . . . The Hostess tells the guest to come in. While the hostess talks to the newcomer, two young men, Georges and Misha, argue about a dancer they have seen. Misha goes into raptures over her "classical figure." Georges will have none of it and is soon joined by the Hostess, who expresses her disapproval. . . . Georges and Misha continue their argument, and Georges calls Misha a dreamer. . . . A Young Man runs up to a man, in whom "it is easy to recognize the one who led off the Stranger." The Young Man says that she is waiting. Then, according to the stage directions, "everything becomes uncommonly strange. It is as if everyone suddenly remembered that somewhere the very same words had been pronounced and in the same order." At this juncture, the Poet enters. The Hostess greets him . . . and then asks the Poet to read. The Poet's reading, however, is interrupted by the arrival of the Stranger, who calls herself Maria. The Young Man and his friend recognize her and the former quietly slips out, making excuses as he leaves. The Hostess then asks the Poet to continue with his reading, but he declines. Instead, he rises and paces the room, trying to remember something. . . . It then appears that the Poet has finally remembered, but as he begins to walk toward the Stranger, the Astronomer gets in his way. The Host and Hostess invite everyone to go into the dining room. As the other guests file out of the drawing room, the Astronomer tells the Poet of a paper he has delivered on the falling star Maria. The Poet, according to the stage directions, "has forgotten everything." The Hostess urges them along from the threshold, but then notices that Maria is nowhere to found. Outside the window, where Maria had been standing, a star now shines. And there falls a "blue snow, just as blue as the dress coat of the Astronomer, who has vanished." With these disappearances, the play ends.[3]

This synopsis brings out a few of the major themes and concerns of the play. The first question is that of the identity of the unknown woman. It is clear that she is to be seen not as some real person but as the incarnation of the desires, dreams, and hopes of various characters. For the poet, who can be understood as Blok's parodic self-portrait, she represents the symbolist dream of the eternal feminine. For the Seminarian, she is a dancer, for the Gentleman, a prostitute, for the Astrologer/Astronomer she is a metaphor for lost illusions, for Georges and Misha she is Isadora Duncan, and for the party Hostess she is another guest. In all cases she is a screen for desire, be it sexual, voyeuristic, philosophical, or symbolic. Her actual essence, if she has any, remains as much a mystery at the end as it was at the beginning. Desire, as the play's central focus, extends to the audience as well, whose desire, at least at the outset, is to solve the mystery of the unknown woman's identity.

All the fragmentary stories about her presented in the play can be boiled down into two groups, one emphasizing her prosaic and the other her lyric potential. Although Westphalen does not mention the fact in his synopsis, this balance between lyric and prosaic elements can be found on other levels of the play as well, reinforced by the dramatic structure. Thus, visions 1 and 3 are in prose, while vision 2 is in verse. Yet, insofar as visions 1 and 3 are structured as imperfect mirror images of one another, they share a traditionally poetic structure. The "poetic" vision 2, on the contrary, tells a completely prosaic story as the unknown woman walks off into the night, presumably to seduce her gentleman admirer, leaving the dreamers behind to lament their fate. Thus, one overarching interpretation of the play would be that it is about what happens when lyric and prosaic worldviews collide and clash.

Desire is also woven into the fabric of the play through the overlapping triangular "love plots" always involving a woman and two men. These can be as simple as the argument between Georges and Misha in which the dancer plays the role of mere placeholder; they can be more complex and competitive as between Maria, the Blue One, and the Gentlemen; or they can be primarily philosophical/artistic, as in the case of the Poet, the Astronomer, and the star/Maria. Such triangular love plots are, of course, the stock in trade of traditional European drama, both in its classical and commedia dell'arte forms. Triangular love arrangements were also exceptionally common in the symbolist milieu in which Blok moved.[4] In this case, the love triangle, especially one in which two men compete for a single woman, helps to knit the dramatic, autobiographical, and subtextual layers of Blok's play into a powerful whole. How might an intertextually inflected reading help us to see further into the play of these and other elements in the drama?

Let us begin our discussion by considering the question of self-reference in relation to *The Unknown Woman*. In our examination of *The Living Corpse*, we had occasion to speak of the way self-reference can be part of an intertextual theatrical strategy. In that case, however, it played a limited role. In the present instance the identity of the titles of the play and a poem suggests a much more intimate connection. The poem is one of Blok's most popular, and it was appreciated almost immediately after its appearance.[5]

The Unknown Woman

In the evenings above the restaurants
The sultry air is wild and still,
And the decaying breath of spring
Carries drunken shouting.

In the distance, above the dusty lanes
And the boredom of summer homes,
The baker's gold sign barely shines
And a child's crying is heard.

And each night, beyond the crossing gates,
With bowler hats tipped rakishly,
The practiced wits stroll with the ladies
Among the drainage ditches.

Out on the lake, oarlocks creak
And a woman lets out a squeal,
While up in the sky, inured to it all,
The moon's disk senselessly leers.

And each night, my solitary friend
Is reflected in my glass,
Made meek and reeling, like myself,
By the astringent, mysterious liquid.

And drowsy servants lounge about
Beside the adjacent tables
While drunks with rabbit eyes cry out
"In vino veritas!"

And each night at a certain hour
(Or am I only dreaming it?),
A girl's figure, swathed in silk,
Moves across the misty window.

And slowly passing among the drunks,
Always alone, unescorted,
Wafting a breath of perfume and mist,
She takes a table by the window.

And an air of ancient legend
Wreaths her resilient silks,
Her hat with its funereal plumes,
And her slender ringed hand.

And entranced by this strange nearness,
I look through her dark veil,
And see an enchanted shore
And an enchanted horizon.

Deep secrets are entrusted to me,
Someone's sun is in my care,
And at every turn, astringent wine
Pierces my soul.

And drooping ostrich plumes
Waver in my brain,
And fathomless blue eyes
Bloom on the distant shore.

A treasure lies in my soul,
And the key belongs to me alone!
You are correct, you drunken fiend!
I know it: wine brings truth.

In the words of Blok's biographer, Avril Pyman, "[T]he fascination of the poem, impossible to convey in translation, is in its effortless combination of a hopeless reality, in which even Nature is unensouled and flat, with a mystical insight leading, through many shifting dimensions, to a suggestion of unfathomable depths."[6] This combination is achieved in the mind and words of the poem's speaker, and as such the poem has a clear solipsistic focus. The reader is meant not to identify him- or herself with the speaker, but rather to reexperience the psychological state presented in the poem.

Let us assume, for the moment at least, that most members of Blok's audience (both in 1906 and subsequently) have encountered the poem before they discover the play. This is not at all an unreasonable assumption, as the poem is one of Blok's most frequently anthologized pieces, while the play is by no means as well known. We can also assume that, with certain variations, they would find Pyman's overall interpretation of the poem convincing. Would they expect to see a simple dramatic transposition of the poem on stage? Or would they expect serious modifications, more than might be required to meet the needs of the new medium? If the latter, are such expectations in fact encoded for them into the fabric of the play?

Some might expect a close intertextual connection to the poem. However, as Timothy Westphalen, the most recent scholar to focus on Blok's dramatic output notes: "the ease with which Blok transformed his poem into a play is all the more striking for the glaring differences between the two. . . . What poem and play share, most importantly, is a number of motifs: the Stranger herself, a bar, alcohol, the inebriation of the persona of the poem and of a character called the Poet in the play. Still, these motifs will appear in a different configuration in the play. Perhaps only in their general thematic contours do the poem and play share very much. . . . beyond this, they have little in common. In fact, 'The Stranger' is only one of several poems that display motifs similar to those in the play."[7] Failing to find a clear intertextual connection with the poem, Westphalen provides instead a subtle analysis of the play by concentrating on doubles, parallelism, and carnival. These are indeed fundamental issues for the play and they do not have much to do with the eponymous poem.

However, I would suggest that Westphalen is wrong to assume that because there are few intertextual connections between the poem and the drama the latter is not a highly intertextual work. First of all, to return to the poem, I would argue that it would be naive to expect the drama to be merely a transposition of the poem. In the first place, of course, for the simple reason that it is not clear what such a transposition of a lyric poem into a dramatic text might be. To be sure, the practice of transposing literary works from other genres into dramatic texts was reasonably common in Russia in the early twentieth century. Thus, the Moscow Art Theatre produced a very successful staging of *The Brothers Karamazov*, Andrei Bely adapted his novel *Petersburg* for the stage, as did Mikhail Bulgakov with his *White Guard*. There are, however, unusual problems in transposing from a lyric poem to a drama.[8] Most obviously, a typical lyric poem has a single speaker and is experienced by a single reader. Even a poem like "The Unknown Woman," which leans toward narrative to a certain extent, remains essentially solipsistic. The poem's narrator speaks to himself and all of the dialogue in the poem takes place in his head. The reader does not know whether the woman described is a figment of his imagination, or a real image transfigured by his imagination. Insofar as drama, even unconventional drama, generally requires some kind of external conflict, some mechanism for bringing more than one perspective to bear on a problem, a lyric requires significant modification if it is to become a play.[9]

In Blok's day, the expectations of readers and potential theatergoers would, have been conditioned by the knowledge that *The Unknown Woman* was not the first play that Blok created around his own lyrics. The far better-known play *Balaganchik* (*The Fairground Booth*) was written in early 1906 and performed at the Kommissarzhevskaia theater under the direction of Meyerhold in 1906. In the case of *The Fairground Booth*, dramatic transposition was simplified considerably because the central personages of the lyric poems that Blok transposed into drama were the traditional figures of Pierrot, Columbine, and Harlequin. These characters had originated in theater rather than in lyric poetry, and, as a result, the stage was their natural home. So the process of creating a stage work around the poems, while complex, necessitated nothing more than bringing the lyric linguistic impulse of Blok's poetry into line with the already existing dramatic potential of his characters. This was clearly not the case with "The Unknown Woman" who had no such dramatic ancestors.

Simultaneously, Blok added a significant note of irony to his *The Fairground Booth* drama. This irony, directed at himself and at those of his symbolist colleagues who in Blok's view had not or were not taking a sufficiently skeptical view of their own ideology, was a major source of controversy when the play appeared. It remains quite easy for contemporary readers to perceive. Given that *The Fairground Booth* is and was far better known than *The Unknown Woman*, it is reasonable to guess that most readers or audience members might expect initially that Blok's dramatic transposition of "The Unknown Woman" would introduce a strong undercurrent of irony into the lyric pathos of the poem. Insofar as the Poet in the drama *The Unknown Woman* can be seen as Blok's alter ego (just as the author figure is in *The Fairground Booth*), I would argue that at least the element of self-irony is used analogously in the two plays. That is to say, both plays take the Blok figure, who in Blok's lyric poetry is generally an unironized presence, and turn him into a figure of ironic ambiguity. In *The Fairground Booth*, the "author" is shown to be completely confused as to the meaning of his text and unable to control either its performance or reception. In *The Unknown Woman*, the inward focus of the poet figure is shown to be neither more nor less valid than other potential views of the woman. As a result, the tone of high (and to some extent self-pitying) seriousness that marks the poem is called into question by the play. In this sense, the relation between lyric and dramatic appears to be analogous in these two "lyric dramas."

At the same time, in using the title *The Unknown Woman* for his play, Blok not only aroused audience expectations regarding possible intertextual relationships between his own poetry and his drama but also in regard to at least one other significant work: the 1883 painting of Ivan Kramskoi entitled *The Unknown Woman* (fig. 3–1). (Kramskoi's painting is entitled "Neizvestnaia" rather than "Neznakomka," but Kramskoi's biographer notes that "among viewers, the name 'Neznakomka' was used with equal frequency as was 'Neizvestnaia' ").[10] This is one of Kramskoi's best-known paintings, and it elicited many responses from the time of its first exhibition. According to Kramskoi's biographer, despite various aesthetic responses to the work, contemporaries agreed about its meaning. As one put it: "it shows a provocatively beautiful woman, all in velvet and fur, throwing you a sneeringly sensuous glance from a luxurious carriage—is this not one of the effluvia of big cities that allow contemptible women dressed in outfits purchased for the price of their female chastity onto the streets?"[11] The Petersburg background, the combination of beauty with sleaze, and the ambiguous relation between the viewer and the subject of the gaze is, therefore, analogous in the poem "The Unknown Woman" and Kramskoi's painting. As a result, the expectations evoked by the title are,

Fig. 3-1.
I. N. Kramskoi, *The Unknown Woman* (Neizvestnaia), 1883. Tretiakov Gallery, Moscow

as it were, doubled for those having knowledge of the painting.

There is, however, one difference between the two and it is crucial to understanding the play. Kramskoi, one of the founders and leading representatives of the so-called Wanderers, was essentially a realist painter, while Blok is undoubtedly a symbolist poet, at least at this period. There can be many definitions of realism in the visual arts, but in the Russian context it has less to do with an attempt at a photographic replication of the real world than it does with the possibility of telling a story. A Russian realist painting, in whatever genre, is an implied narrative. In this case, as we look at the woman in Kramskoi's painting, we can hardly resist telling one or more stories about her; the visual work elicits a strong narrative undercurrent. In this sense, the painting, while close to Blok's poem in terms of subject matter, evokes a different set of expectations. The play's spectator might guess from the clash of elements encoded in its title that it will present a kind of synthesis between the essentially lyrical impulse of Blok's poetry and the essentially novelistic impulse of the painting. As we will see, this hypothesis is a helpful one for reading "The Unknown Woman," for such a synthesis does indeed play itself out in a number of ways in the drama: on the level of language (prose vs. verse), and in structure (linear vs. circular), theme (reality vs. illusion), and characterization (Madonna or whore in the person of Maria).

Furthermore, the guess that the potential double reference of the title represents a coded sign that the play will map out an attempt to prosaicize Blok's theme is enforced by the two epigraphs inserted between the title and the first "vision" of the play. The epigraphs themselves are both drawn from Dostoevsky's novel *The Idiot*. The first is taken from the novel's third chapter, the scene in which Prince Myshkin sees Nastasia Filippovna for the first time, in a photograph. "The portrait depicted a woman of truly unusual beauty. She was photographed in a black silk dress of an extremely simple and elegant cut; her hair, evidently dark-blond, was done in a simple, domestic style; her eyes were dark, deep, her brow thoughtful; the expression on her face was passionate and somehow arrogant. Her face was somewhat thin, perhaps, and pale . . ."[12] The second epigraph is drawn from part I, chapter 9, and is excerpted from the first conversation between Myshkin and Nastasia Filippovna. "But how did you know it was I? Where have you seen me before? Really, what's going on here, apparently I've seen him somewhere?" . . . "I have apparently seen you somewhere, too?" "Where, where?" "I have definitely seen your eyes somewhere. . . . But this cannot be! I'm just . . . I've never even been here. Perhaps in a dream. . . . " (p. 39).

Regarding the specific material chosen by Blok, the epigraphs set up a number of new expectations. The first one connects the unknown woman of Blok's poem with the femme fatale theme that runs through most of Dostoevsky's later work. The second epigraph, with is emphasis on the issue of déjà vu and the question of what constitutes reality and what the dream world again seems to echo and to amplify some of the concerns of Blok's lyric. In particular, one of the central concerns of the novel is the relationship of any and every image to reality: Nastasia Filippovna's photograph stands in metonymically for all these moments and that seems to be at least one of the contexts in which Blok is invoking the novel here. Of crucial importance to Dostoevsky's novel are those liminal situations during which, as in an early photograph, a person seems uncannily immanent although he or she is not physically present. Most readers of Dostoevsky will probably recall a number of scenes in *The Idiot* in which characters are unable to ascertain whether they are seeing a person or a photograph-like image of that person.

Perhaps not surprisingly, the most striking one involves Myshkin and Nastasia Filippovna. After the sleepless night during which Ippolit reads his confession, the Prince walks into the Pavlovsk Park early in the morn- ing and falls asleep.[13] "He had many dreams and they were all disturbed; at times they made him tremble. At last a woman came to him; he knew her, he knew her and suffered in knowing her. He could name her and point her out, but, strange to say, her face seemed completely different from the one he had always known, and he felt revulsion against recognizing her as the same woman. There was such remorse and horror in this face that it seemed she must be a terrible criminal."[14] As was the case with the photographed face, the dream image hides an apparent mystery, one that can be read only in an absent face that appears as an image. When the embodied face actually appears, it generally fails to register the eeriness that the substitute (either a photograph or a dream image cognized as a photograph) makes legible. All of this is related, of course, to the play's central question regarding the nature of desire. The mediated photograph helps us to recognize that we do not desire an object per se, but rather the image of that desire, an image that frequently enough is of our own creation and has little connection with the actual object.

Simultaneously, the epigraphs recall to us the fact that *The Idiot* is not merely a novel but a Petersburg novel in particular. It therefore evokes the whole tradition of literature about "that most unreal of cities" going back as far as Pushkin. For Dostoevsky, however, although Pushkin may be the founder of the tradition, the crucial predecessor is Nikolai Gogol. And I would argue that the reference to Dostoevsky's Petersburg novel by Blok should almost automatically bring up in his readers' minds the possibility of a Gogolian subtext. This suspicion is immediately confirmed, for in the stage directions to the first act, we read the following description of the bar in which the action takes place.

> Behind the bar onto which has been hoisted a barrel with a gnome and the inscription "Mug-Goblet," are a pair who look completely alike: each with a tuft of parted hair and in a green apron; but the PROPRIETOR's mustache curls downward [*usy vniz*] while his brother's, the WAITER's curls upwards [*usy vverkh*]. By one window, at a small table, sits a drunken OLD MAN—the spitting image of VERLAINE; by the other, a clean-shaven, pale man—the spitting image of HAUPTMANN. (p. 41)

Two Gogol stories are evoked pretty clearly here. The first is "The Tale of How Ivan Ivanovich Quarreled with Ivan Nikiforovich." In that story, part of the *Mirgorod* collection, as a part of his description of the two Ivans, Gogol writes: "Ivan Ivanovich's head looks like a radish, tail downwards [*khvostom vniz*]; Ivan Nikiforovich's is like a radish, tail up [*khvostom vverkh*]."[15] This reference, as it turns out, is something of a red herring, for nothing about Blok's play seems to connect to Gogol's work. What it does do, however, is signal the more important but somewhat more hidden Gogol connection that follows in the next line.

In Gogol's famous "Nevsky prospekt," we may recall that one of Gogol's heroes encounters two foreigners who both are and are not famous writers: "Before him stood Schiller—not the Schiller who wrote "William Tell" and "The History of the Thirty Years War," but the well-known Schiller, master tinker of Meshchanskii street. Right next to Schiller stood Hoffman—not the writer Hoffman but a rather good shoemaker."[16] Just as the "poet" in this play both is and is not Blok, and the play itself both is and is not lyric and novel, the two men in Blok's tavern who both are and are not Verlaine and Hauptman are analogues to Gogol's craftsmen who both are and are not famous German writers. And in the cases of the characters, the comic displacements signal not merely humor, but a global concern of the works discussed here with the relationship between reality and illusion. Recall again that the Dostoevsky epigraph specifically concerned this problem. At the same time, the reference to Hauptman may also have an ironic autobiographical ring. In his, admittedly written much later, memoir, *Reminiscences of Aleksandr Blok*, Andrei Bely tells of a conversation with a mutual friend of his and Blok's (A. S. Petrovsky) soon after he had met Blok for the first time. Bely recalls having been surprised by Blok's external appearance and to have told Petrovsky that Blok "looks like a carrot, or . . . like Hauptmann."[17] The assumption that Petrovsky eventually told Blok of this description may help to explain the combination of Gogol's imagery (the radish here turned into a carrot) with Hauptman to make an ironic, and very Gogolian autobiographical insertion into his play.

As we see, from the first pages of Blok's play a complicated web of intertexts has been established that connects the work first of all to the lyrical tradition in which Blok found himself, to Blok's own biography, and to the Russian prose tradition of the Petersburg tale as exemplified by Gogol and Dostoevsky. That crucial intertextual references appear in epigraphs and stage directions underscores one of the central differences between Blok's use of intertextuality and that of Tolstoy or Chekhov. In the cases we have considered previously, the audience was the ultimate addressee of the intertextual messages. But in those plays the characters were the primary vehicles for intertextual references, and what is more they themselves recognized to a certain extent the intertextual game of which they were part. The effect was to theatricalize Tolstoy's and Chekhov's plays, which otherwise might have been too easy to read and perform as "slices of life" about "real people." In the case of Blok's theater, there is no danger of the audience coming to a realist interpretation, and no need for the characters to recognize literary parallels with their "real" lives. The use of epigraphs, which are not available in any way to the characters of the play, points up the greater artificiality of Blok's theatrical practice. It also creates a dilemma for the director, who must figure out a convincing way to provide the epigraphs for an audience in the theater.

It is worth noting that Vsevolod Meyerhold, in his 1914 staging of the play, emphasized the nonmimetic aspects of the work. As described by a contemporary eyewitness:

> The opening scene takes place in a tavern. A number of actors with no parts in the play acted as "proscenium servants" with the task of scene shifting. Dressed in special unobtrusive costumes and moving rhythmically, they brought on tables, stools, a bar, and to the rear raised a green curtain on bamboo poles. . . . When the scene ended there was a roll of drums and the servants who had been holding up the curtain walked forward, stretching the curtain above the actors and then lowering it to hide them from the audience whilst they removed all the properties from the stage . . . [18]

We can say that the overt concern of the Dostoevsky epigraphs leads the reader to recognize a somewhat hidden connection with Gogol's short stories, particularly "Nevsky Prospekt." Indeed, it would not be an exaggeration to claim that Blok's play is best read as a lyrical variation on a Gogolian theme, for the more one looks at the two works together the more striking the similarities become.[19] Gogol's story begins, as does Blok's play, with a scene that paints a complicated portrait of a real place in St. Petersburg. Blok's stage directions, which call for large picture windows through which many passers-by can be seen, provide a framing device similar to Gogol's famous introductory paragraphs that take the pulse of Nevsky's passers-by. Although these passers-by are many, Gogol's narrative focuses especially on the young artist Piskarev. Like Blok's Poet, Piskarev is an impressionable and sensitive young man obsessed by a vision of a lovely woman. The woman, who turns out to be a prostitute, is referred to three times in Gogol's text as "*neznakomka*."[20] Just as Blok's play is built around a "low" first scene that is later repeated in "high" society, Gogol's story presents a double vision of the prostitute.[21] In the first scene the poet enters the brothel in which she works and is shocked by the degradation he finds. That scene is later repeated in the poet's dreams but transposed to an evening in the finest society.

What is more, the last page of Gogol's story is precisely devoted to the question of the relationship between illusion and reality. "O, do not believe Nevsky prospect! I always wrap myself up more tightly in my coat when I walk along it, and I try not to look the objects I meet in the face. It is all illusion, all dreams, everything is different from what it appears to be."[22] This close connection to Gogol's story mediated via Dostoevsky's novel reveals not just similarities in plot and theme, but uncovers one other desire—the desire of the text to place itself within the Petersburg tradition of Russian literature. That tradition, which stretches back at the very least to Pushkin, emphasizes the irreality of the city, and the capriciousness and instability of relationships within it. The desire to connect Russian symbolism to that tradition (also manifest in Andrei Bely's celebrated 1916 novel *Petersburg*) can be seen as part and parcel of a desire to connect symbolism with a central thread of Russian literary history. Given that this thread is primarily narrative rather than lyric, Blok's desire to write himself into the Petersburg tradition points to a more general desire encoded in the play's web of intertextual relationships to broaden out from the lyric.

This desire helps to answer one other question about Blok's dramatic work in general. After all, one wants to ask, why would Blok, an extremely successful lyric poet, have wanted to write dramas in the first place? One answer can be found in Blok's own description of what his lyric dramas meant to him.[23] In a letter to Meyerhold as the director was preparing to stage *Balaganchik*, Blok wrote: "You must believe that it is necessary for me to be near your theater, necessary for me that "Balaganchik" should appear there now, in this purging moment when I am leaving lyric isolation."[24] As we noted above, solipsism is undoubtedly a danger for the lyric poet, and one can appreciate why Blok might have felt this to be confining, particularly after the 1905 revolution when the whole country had seemingly become interested in collective sociopolitical ideas.

There is strong evidence that *The Unknown Woman* was an equally important attempt to escape lyrical isolation. We know, for example, that the play was not Blok's only attempt to illustrate to contemporaries that *The Unknown Woman* existed as a narrative outside the poem. Zhenya Ivanov describes a walk taken with Blok in Ozerki (a resort north of St. Petersburg) at about this time:

> We arrived. Walked alongside the lake where the "oarlocks creaked" and the "women squealed." We walked as far as Shuvalovo. There's a café there. We had a cup of coffee in the café. Then Sasha, with a sort of tenderness to me reminiscent of Virgil's to Dante, pointed out the gilded "Krendel" on the café sign. He did the honors of the place most lovingly. As though he'd wanted to put my feet on the very way he had trodden that evening when the Unknown Woman had first appeared.[25]

Blok thus apparently emphasized to his friends that in creating the poem he had condensed a story that perhaps would have been more effectively told in another genre.

I would suggest that it is precisely the inability of lyric poetry to embody the "objective" reality of a situation that Blok understood as lyric isolation; it was this same desire that led Blok to bring his friends to the spot at which the Unknown Woman had "really" appeared to him and to attempt to embody a version of that situation in his play. At the same time, it would be a mistake to think that the play was meant to reenact in any kind of unmediated way some event in Blok's life. That could have been, perhaps, something he attempted to realize for a few friends, but he was not so naive as to think that another literary genre could be capable of reproducing reality, nor would he have likely wanted to do this had it been possible.

In this context we can perhaps see another reason for the choice of Dostoevsky's novel as Blok's central subtext. For Dostoevsky, of all Russian prose writers, is the most "dramatic." His novels are filled with scenes that seem as if they should be in a play, and it is no accident that his fiction became the source of numerous scripts for plays, operas, and films.[26] If one of Blok's goals in "rewriting" his earlier poem was to make it less isolated, another goal was to rewrite Dostoevsky to make him more lyrical. The drama is the intermediate form that allows for the confrontation of a lyrical subject with the prosaic tradition.

One final question we need to ask in relation to Dostoevsky is why

Blok should have chosen to take the particular epigraphs he did from *The Idiot*. In her exhaustive treatment of intertextuality and *The Unknown Woman*, Schamma Schahadat considers the relationship of the play to early cinema. Building on work done by Hansen-Löve, Lotman, and Gasparov, Schahadat notes Blok's attraction to the low cultural qualities of the early cinema, and finds thematic parallels between the play and a number of contemporary French films by Georges Meliès. Specifically, she points to the films *La Rêve de l'astronome* (1898) and *Le Voyage dans la Lune* (1902), noting specific plot connections between the films and Blok's play. What is more, she notes some suggestive ways in which the play mimics film techniques, particularly in the obviously cinematic fade-in and fade-out techniques described in the stage directions to bridge the first and second "visions" of the play.[27] To this I would add only that the cinematic connection provides one more motivation for the first epigraph chosen from *The Idiot*. After all, there are a number of scenes in which Nastasia Filippovna is described in Dostoevsky's novel, any one of which could potentially have been chosen by Blok as his epigraph. He opted to use the one in which she appears in a photograph, however, thus emphasizing the connection of the novel to early photography.[28] The epigraph thus functions as an indication that indeed a cinematic reference should be present in *The Unknown Woman*, for insofar as Dostoevsky's novel can be read as an exploration of the then-new art of still photography, so Blok's play is a meditation on some potentials inherent in the new art of cinematography.

Finally, we need to explore the ways in which other aspects of Blok's biography, and particularly his relations with Andrei Bely, are woven into the dramatic and subtextual structure of the play. If we look again at the central subtexts for *The Unknown Woman* and ask what they have in common in addition to the Petersburg motif, we can see that both are about the ways in which women destroy the comradeship (or potential comradeship) of the two male protagonists. In the case of Gogol's story this plotline is only rudimentary. The two male heroes, Piskarev and Pirogov, are described as "chums" (*priiateli*) as they walk together down Nevsky Prospect. And chums they might have remained had not they seen two women whose charms lead them off in opposite directions never to see each other again. If, for Gogol, this aspect of the story was of secondary importance (although, as Simon Karlinsky has demonstrated, plots of this sort are quite significant for Gogol in general),[29] for Dostoevsky's novel it is absolutely central. There is no question that although both men are sexually attracted to Nastasia Filippovna, they are at least equally attracted to each other (although given their own backgrounds and the time, they do not appear to perceive this in a conscious way). Thus, as Nina Pelikan Straus puts it in her insightful article "Flights from *The Idiot*'s Womanhood": "Her transfiguration in death is the opportunity for Myshkin's and Rogozhin's final male bonding, revealing how she has served as 'traffic' between them."[30] It would not even be too much to add that perhaps Nastasia's death forces the two men to recognize their attraction to each other (hidden by their competition for her favors while she was alive), and that it is in part this realization that pushes Myshkin over the edge into insanity and Rogozhin into incoherent illness.

As has been noted by many biographers, Blok writes *The Unknown Woman* precisely at the moment when his own friendship with Andrei Bely was unraveling because of Bely's recognition that he was in love with Blok's wife, Liubov' Mendeleeva.[31] Blok and Bely had met only in 1903 (although they had corresponded for some time previous to this), but immediately felt a strong affinity for one another. Although Bely's memoirs place primary emphasis on the intellectual attractions of the two men, even this Soviet-era work does not completely hide the evidence of latent sexual attraction. While Blok did not leave an autobiography, there is evidence that this attraction between the leading poet and leading theoretician of the second generation of symbolists was shared. At the beginning, Blok's wife clearly played the role of mediator of the relationship not so much by her intellect as by her physical presence. As Bely began to recognize his desire for Liubov', however, the carefully balanced triangular relationship began to crack. From Blok's point of view, it might well have seemed that the situation of male understanding and desire mediated by a woman was collapsing.

In any case, one can certainly read the ending of the second act of the play, in which the poet (Blok's alter ego) and the astrologer (whose theoretically inclined nature recalls that of Bely, the same Bely whose poetry collection *Zoloto v lazuri* [Gold in Azure] links easily with a celestial thematics) spar and then come together after the "unknown woman's" disappearance, as an expression of a wish for a union of the two men at the expense of Liubov'.

ASTROLOGER.

Well, grief like yours will soon pass!
For you need only to write
Your verses as lengthy as possible!
What do you have to cry about?

POET.

And as for you, Mr. Astrologer,
All you need is to take your scrolls
And inscribe for the schooling of students:
"Maria has fallen – a star!"

(*Both mourn beneath the sky-blue snow. They vanish in it . . .*) (p. 57).

Unlike *The Idiot*, however, Blok's work does not end with an image of two men coming together at the expense and in the absence of a woman. In Dostoevsky's work, as Josten Børtnes has argued:

> A queer reading of *The Idiot* reveals the presence of homosexual relations in the novel's universe as well as in the culture that produced it. The novel's ending demonstrates to what extent patriarchal power relations have been structured as heterosexual, and how the schizogenic force of homophobia that sustains the novel's patriarchal order will inevitably cause its own disintegration in the end.[32]

The ending of the play, then, in which the woman disappears leaving the astronomer and the poet (the alter egos of Bely and Blok respectively) behind, represents both a rewriting of the ending of Dostoevsky's novel and perhaps a wish fulfillment on the part of Blok. Maria, the unknown woman, manages once again to elude both the poet and the astrologer, disappearing from the fashionable party where she appeared unexpectedly amid the guests. This time, however, rather than leaving the two men together as he did at the end of the second act, and as he perhaps wished would be the case in life, Blok leaves only his alter ego behind, his condition clearly recalling that of Myshkin at the end of Dostoevsky's novel: "*He turns toward the depths of the room. Stares hopelessly. On his face—anguish; in his eyes—emptiness and gloom. He reels from the terrible strain.* **But he has forgotten everything.**"[33] The fate of the other members of the triad is ambiguous at best, as the final stage directions attest: "*There is no one by the dark curtain. A bright star burns outside the window. Sky-blue snow is falling, the same sky-blue as the uniform of the vanished* ASTROLOGER." That is, the unknown woman, still mysterious, has apparently regained her place in the heavens, while the astrologer has vanished from the scene, precisely as Bely did in late 1906.

If we now return to the questions we posed at the outset, we can see that an intertextual reading of the play deepens and clarifies Blok's work. The unknown woman, positioned as she is between Blok's own work and her prototypes in Dostoevsky's novel, in Gogol's story, and in Kramskoi's painting, illustrates the central function of the drama for Blok. It allowed an escape from the dangerous solipsism of the lyric by moving in the direction of narrative (the Petersburg narrative in particular), as well as toward the central theme of this particular drama, desire; and to the central desire of the play: to encode Blok's personal drama in an overarching literary and cultural framework.

NOTES

1. As noted, the title can also be translated as "The Stranger." In Russian, however, the word is clearly gendered as a female personage, so I have preferred to use the more suggestive, albeit longer and clumsier, "Unknown Woman."
2. For an English translation of the play, see *Eight Twentieth-Century Russian Plays*, trans. and ed. Timothy Langen and Justin Weir, pp. 39–64.
3. Westphalen, pp. 52–54.
4. See various chapters in Paperno and Grossman's *Creating Life: The Aesthetic Utopia of Russian Modernism*, especially those by Olga Matich and Joan Grossman.
5. See Pyman, 1:240–244, for a discussion of the contemporary reception of this poem. Insofar as the poem was well-received and would have been well-known to contemporaries, this distinguishes the intertextual effect caused by self-reference in this play from that in Blok's most famous drama "The Fairground Booth" (*Balaganchik*). That play is also connected to one of the author's own poems, but it is a rather obscure one.
6. Pyman, 1:241.
7. Westphalen, pp. 50–52.
8. See Iampolski, pp. 51–121 for a discussion of the use of lyrics in early cinema.
9. A year or so after the publication of Blok's play, his fellow symbolist Fedor Sologub came up with an ingenious and much talked-about solution to this problem in his article "*Teatr odnoi voli*," which appeared in the collection *Teatr. Kniga o novom teatre*.
10. Porudominsky, p. 222.

11. Quoted in Porudominsky, p. 223.

12. *The Unknown Woman*, in Langen and Weir, p. 39. Further citations from this play will be made in the main text by reference to this translation.

13. Dostoevsky, 8:352. Slightly earlier in the novel Ippolit also describes a scene in which a face appears (Rogozhin's) and he is unable to ascertain whether or not there is a person attached to it. Dostoevsky 8:340–341.

14. This scene is repeated a bit later in the novel. ". . . again he had an oppressive dream, and again the same criminal woman came to him. Again she looked at him with tears shining on her long lashes, again she beckoned him to follow her and again he awoke, as before with an agonizing remembrance of her face." Dostoevsky, 8:377.

15. Gogol, 2:178.

16. Gogol, 3:30.

17. Bely, 1995, p. 58.

18. The description is by Znosko-Borovsky and is quoted at length in Meyerhold, 1969, pp. 116–117.

19. For a different interpretation of the relationship between the play and the works of Dostoevsky and Gogol, see Schahadat, pp. 191–213.

20. Gogol, 3:14–15.

21. For an interesting discussion on the general connections between Gogol's and Blok's views of women, see Andrei Bely, *Masterstvo Gogolia* (Ann Arbor, MI: Ardis, 1982), pp. 294–297.

22. Gogol, 3:38.

23. Blok wrote three lyric dramas in 1906, including *Balaganchik, The Unknown Woman*, and *The King on the Square*.

24. Quoted in Medvedev, p. 15.

25. Quoted in Pyman, 1:243. Translation modified to agree with the usages in this chapter.

26. For more on this topic see Alexander Burry, "Transposition as Interpretation: Dostoevsky in the Twentieth Century." (PhD dissertation, Northwestern University, 2001.)

27. See Schahadat, pp. 243–251. The cinematographic nature of Blok's play was already apparent to Andrei Bely, although he saw this in fairly negative terms: "a series of cinematographic associations, non-linkages—that is the meaning of Blok's drama." Andrei Bely, *Vospominaniia o Bloke*, p. 336.

28. For a discussion about Dostoevsky's use of photography in *The Idiot*, see my article "*The Idiot* as Photograph," in *History of Photography* (26:3) Autumn 2002, pp. 205–215.

29. See Karlinsky, 1976.

30. Knapp, p. 113. For more on this issue, see Børtnes.

31. To my knowledge, this subject was first treated in depth by Konstantin Mochulsky in his biography *Aleksandr Blok*, published posthumously in 1948.

32. Børtnes, p. 120.

33. Blok, *The Unknown Woman*, both citations p. 64 (emphasis mine).

CHAPTER 4
Intertextual Relations in *Petrushka*

THE BALLET *PETRUSHKA*, in contrast to most of the other dramatic works considered in this volume, in which intertextual play can be ascribed in the final analysis to a single author—albeit one who may well tap into intertextual sources of which he is not consciously aware—is a work by multiple authors.[1] As a consequence, the play of intertextual expectations is frequently generated by the various sources and interpretations of those sources by the project's three central collaborators. The resulting work displays, not surprisingly, an exceptionally complex web of intertexts whose interrelationship produced one of the great theatrical works of the twentieth century.

The initial stimulus for the ballet was a programmatic piano piece that Igor Stravinsky played for Sergei Diaghilev in Switzerland sometime in the autumn (probably October) of 1910. However, Stravinsky had not worked out a full story line, and Diaghilev, always on the lookout for new material, suggested that he enlist the artist and critic Alexandre Benois as a collaborator on a new ballet based on this work. Stravinsky and Benois exchanged a number of letters in which they worked out the details of the libretto in late 1910 and early 1911, and completed it sometime before April of that year. After the libretto was finished to the satisfaction of Stravinsky and Benois, it was up to the choreographer Michel Fokine to bring their ideas to life. Rehearsals for the ballet began in Rome in April 1911, and it was here that the details were filled in. There is, unfortunately, no written record of Fokine's contribution to the libretto. His copy of the score contains some annotations for a couple of scenes, but for the most part the choreography was produced in the course of rehearsals. In this sense, although Fokine was never credited with being an author of the libretto, he had a major role in interpreting the fairly conceptual text that Stravinsky and Benois provided.

In part as a result of this triple authorship, *Petrushka* points to a number of sources and meanings simultaneously, and each one of these creates what could be called a field of expectations for the spectator. Each time a motif appears that can clearly be defined as belonging to one field or another, the audience expects to find it developed further. Of course, for a knowledgeable audience, it takes only a small bit of cultural material to evoke a large field of expectations. In *Petrushka*, most of the time anyway, the line suggested is not developed in a straightforward manner but is instead modified or distorted through contact with other motifs, each carrying its own field of expectations. Sometimes the layers mesh smoothly, while at other times jarring ambiguity results. In the course of the ballet, through the frequent appearance of certain motifs, a pattern begins to emerge. In *Petrushka* the expectational fields tend to be drawn from both poles of what are normally seen as mutually exclusive binary oppositions such as high culture/popular culture, comedy/tragedy, realism/grotesque, serious drama/parody. By invoking both simultaneously, *Petrushka* aims to question the very nature of such binary oppositions.

The distortions that result can be likened to the interaction of two musical themes played in counterpoint. The listener continues to hear the two original themes while their interaction can produce the illusion of a third theme. To illustrate how the analogy works in practice, we might mention, for example, that the juxtaposition of high- and low-cultural material in the ballet fails to lead to the annihilation of one or the other; instead, we get a product with the intellectual weight of a serious work of art and with the unpretentious exuberance of a more popular art form: not either/or but both/and. The picture is further complicated by the fact that many textual motifs can evoke more than one field. The same bit can be seen, for example, as serious or parodic, depending on which set of interpretive criteria a spectator chooses to invoke. When we consider the libretto as a whole we will return to this question, but before we can analyze the whole product it is necessary to return to the individual themes in our counterpoint, in this case to our separate sources, to capture the field of expectations evoked by each of them. The subtexts on which the ballet is based can be broken down into three broad categories. They are derived from popular culture, modernist theater and drama, and nineteenth-century opera and ballet.

The Popular Culture Origins of *Petrushka*:
Petrushka and the Petrushka Play

Much has been made of the relationship of this ballet to popular culture, both on the level of the music and the libretto. Richard Taruskin has treated the former issue exhaustively.[2] Regarding the libretto, the main reasons for considering this problem center on comments by Stravinsky and Benois, and on the field of expectations created by the ballet's title. In his *Autobiography*, Stravinsky described the genesis of a work for piano and orchestra that later became the ballet. In an oft-quoted passage he says: "I had in my mind a distinct picture of a puppet, suddenly endowed with life, exasperating the patience of the orchestra with diabolical cascades of arpeggios. The orchestra in turn retaliates with menacing trumpet blasts. The outcome is a terrific noise which reaches its climax and ends in the sorrowful and querulous collapse of the poor puppet." He goes on to relate his search for a title for this work. "One day I leapt for joy. I had indeed found my title—*Petroushka*, the immortal and unhappy hero of every fair in all countries."[3]

A similar theme is sounded by Benois in his *Reminiscences of the Russian Ballet*. He relates that Diaghilev wrote him with the news that Stravinsky had "played a sort of Russian Dance and another piece which he had named *Petrouchka's Cry* . . . but no story had as yet been devised. They had only conceived the idea of representing the St. Petersburg carnival and of including in it a performance of Petrouchka, the Russian Punch and Judy show."[4] Then he adds: "As to Petrouchka in person, I immediately had the feeling that 'it was a duty I owed to my old friend' to immortalise him on the real stage. I was still more tempted by the idea of depicting the Butter Week Fair on the stage, the dear *balagani* which were the great delight of my childhood."[5] However, notwithstanding the claims of the two main authors that the Russian Petrushka play was an important influence on the libretto, closer examination shows that this influence has been exaggerated.

What, in fact, is the Russian Petrushka play, where does it come from, and of what does its plot consist?—that is, what subtextual expectations would have been evoked in a Russian audience when they encountered the ballet's title? The first record of puppet theater in Russia appears in the journal of Adam Olearius, a seventeenth-century Dutch traveler. "Their dancing-bear impresarios have comedians with them, who, among other things, arrange farces employing puppets. These comedians tie a blanket around their bodies and spread it above their heads, thus creating a portable theater or stage with which they can run about the streets, and on top of which they can give puppet shows."[6] Until recently, it was assumed that what Olearius described was a "Petrushka" play and that, therefore, the show is an ancient Russian tradition. More recent research, however, indicates that this is not so; instead, it seems that the characteristic Russian glove-puppet show starring Petrushka was an early nineteenth-century import.[7] Be that as it may, Russian audiences of the late nineteenth and early twentieth centuries considered Petrushka to be a native and ancient tradition.

The plotlines of such puppet shows remained basically the same whenever they were performed, although a certain amount of variation was permissible in secondary scenes. Petrushka decides to marry and sets off to buy a horse to give as the bride price. He meets a gypsy who tries to sell him an overly frisky horse. Petrushka takes offense, beats the gypsy with his staff (sometimes he kills the gypsy), and takes the horse. He mounts the horse and is thrown, thus necessitating the appearance of a doctor. Petrushka takes the doctor for a quack and beats or kills him with his staff. Then follow a series of confrontations with policemen, military officers, and others, all of which end with Petrushka beating or killing his opponent. The play generally ends with Petrushka being dragged off to hell.[8]

As to the personality of the central character, Petrushka himself, a description by Dostoevsky provides an excellent if somewhat rose-tinted outline: "How trusting he is, how joyful and straightforward, how he wishes not to believe in evil and deceit, how quickly he becomes angry and throws himself against unfairness and how he exults as soon as he whacks someone with his staff."[9] In fact, it would seem that whacking, both verbal and physical, was the most pronounced element of what was, in reality, a cruder and crueler spectacle than Dostoevsky's recollections would have it. As to Petrushka's appearance, it

> was that of a clown in miniature. He was physically deformed, with a hunch-back, distorted physiognomy (all nose and chin with button eyes) shortened thorax, and swinging, useless legs. He carried a powerful club (known in Russian as *dubinka*), with which he was violently active. His moral characteristics were as unbeautiful as his physique, combining gluttony, priapism, psychopathic aggression, cowardice, cupidity and overpowering egotism.[10]

From this description of the action of a typical puppet play and the character of its hero, one thing should be clear: the story of the ballet and that of the traditional puppet show have little in common. The disjunction between the incongruity of the expectations evoked by the ballet's title and the libretto's content seems, at least initially, to have bothered Stravinsky. In a letter to Benois written early in the creative process he noted, with what sounds like an edge of panic, "In my opinion, for the name «Petrushka» in this show there is either too little Petrushka, or at least his role both qualitatively and quantitatively is equivalent to that of the other characters (the Moor and the Ballerina) when in fact there should be more of a concentration on him. Do you agree with me?"[11] Benois, however, appears not to have been concerned by the libretto's lack of connection to the standard Petrushka story. This was not because he did not know the puppet show, but rather because, as was clear in the passage quoted earlier, his own field of expectations upon hearing the title included not so much the puppet play itself as the entire context in which such plays were normally performed.

This initial clash of the expectational fields of the two collaborators and its ultimate resolution is a good example of the nature of the writing process that produced *Petrushka*, a richer, if less pure version of the story than either of the main contributors would have imagined by himself. The extent to which collaboration with Benois enriched and complicated Stravinsky's conception of the story can be seen in a letter Stravinsky sent as he was putting the finishing touches on the ballet in February 1911. "When I was first writing Petrushka's music and did not yet think that three tableaux would grow from his little apartment, I imagined him giving a performance on the Field of Mars. Now, after our collaborative reworking, it turns out quite the opposite."[12] Ultimately, the ballet's title turns out to be something of a red herring. It harks back to Stravinsky's initial design for the project, one in which the role of Petrushka was to have been far more central, while in the final version Benois' wider expectational field emerged as the more important. In order to understand the popular culture subtext of the actual ballet, therefore, we must shift our attention away from the Petrushka play itself and pay more attention to the setting in which such plays were presented.

The Shrovetide Carnival

By the middle of the nineteenth century the typical Russian city-dweller associated the Petrushka play with the carnivals at which it was performed. These occurred twice yearly, the week of Shrovetide and the week after Easter, the former being the more popular. In Petersburg, they took place on the Admiralty Square until 1874. One writer describes them as follows:

> So, on what was, in fact, a small plot which stretched between the building of the General Staff to St. Isaac's, facing Nevsky Prospect with a "backyard" facing the Admiralty, twice a year—each time for one week—there grew up a crowded, colorful and loud festival town which could have been best defined by the words "something for everyone."[13]

From 1875 to 1897 carnivals were held on the Field of Mars, after which they were moved away from the center of town and died out; by 1910 they had become a nostalgic memory. As is frequently the case, the artistic potential of folk art and customs was realized by the bearers of culture only after they had become a memory.

For Benois, the carnival was a source of both nostalgia and inspiration. "The *balagany* [by which he means the whole carnival celebration] on the Field of Mars were a collection of village merrymaking in the city—a big, playful uncontrolled village where we, the gentry children, were taken to 'learn Russia' without realizing it."[14] Nostalgia is clear in an article written slightly later in which he complains of the "strength of some kind of laws which doom to destruction everything in Russian life that is real, unique, colorful and joyful."[15] Stravinsky remembered the carnivals fondly as well. Describing his birthplace he said, "St. Petersburg was also a city of large open piazzas. One of these, the Champs de Mars, might have been the scene of *Petroushka*. The Mardi Gras festivities were centered there and, as puppet shows were part of the carnival entertainment, it was there that I saw my first 'Petroushka.'"[16] As we have already noted, for Benois the traditional setting for the Petrushka play seems to have left a stronger impression than the play itself. As we begin to examine accounts of the carnivals, their importance for the first and fourth tableaux of *Petrushka* becomes obvious.

Contemporary descriptions of the Shrovetide carnival sound almost like plot and prop lists for the first tableau of the ballet:

> An undefined hum hangs in the air. The loud talk of the folk, the shouts of peddlers calling to the public, the sounds of orchestras,

barrel-organs, the squeak of wooden puppets jumping out from behind screens, volleys from shooting galleries, the songs from the carousels—all flowed into one. ... Fox and raccoon coats, coarse wool coats, patterned shawls, velvet jackets, sheepskins, soldiers' helmets and overcoats, ersatz Russian costumes of wetnurses, servants' liveries —all mixed together.

The Field of Mars roars and hums, hums and groans, bathed in a sea of lights all the colors of the rainbow and flowers. . . . And the sounds? This is not sounds, it is a chaos of sounds. It is a gigantic, miraculous formless chaos. A barrel-organ squeaks, a trumpet roars, bells clang, a flute sings, a drum hums, conversation, exclamations, shouts, laughter, cursing, song. There's a holiday carousel, decorated with flags, lit up, decked out, illuminated. And here's a barker with his linen beard, the classic barker, that eternal jester, but a jester who holds the whole crowd in his hands, a jester who has power over them and, with a single word, forces the crowd to laugh, to laugh until they cry . . . [17]

It was this somewhat barbaric but colorful and peculiarly Russian group of sights that formed the frame for an updated version of the Petrushka play. Both Stravinsky and Benois contributed ideas for these scenes. In the first letter that Stravinsky wrote to Benois about the ballet he states: "I have already composed the Shrovetide in the first tableau before the magic trick, and the "Russian dance" after it." [18] He does not give any details, however. Benois, writing back, is much more explicit in his plans for the carnival scene, going so far as to give Stravinsky advice on musical matters:

Now comes general relief and endless happiness; carousels, ice mountains, puppet shows are all illuminated by hundreds of lanterns and a torchlight bacchanale begins. The carousels spin, sound, and ring, and an all-inclusive devilishly-spirited dance takes place on the square. The representatives of the beau monde whip off a kind of cancan-mazurka with great vigor, while the folk gather in a gigantic circle with leaps, leg kicks and a puppet in the shape of a devil. A counterpoint of twenty themes (at least)—ringing, little bells, and maybe even an accordian used as an orchestral instrument. [19]

The final version of this scene pleased Benois particularly. Years later, in his memoirs, he ended his description of the Russian carnival by saying: "This atmosphere is admirably reproduced in the fourth scene of Stravinsky's *Petrushka*."[20]

Of course, as was to be expected, not all the collaborators understood the crowd scenes exactly as Benois did. In an otherwise glowing article on the ballet, written immediately after its premiere, Benois complained: "in general the typical Russian scenes didn't come out too well for him [Fokine]. This Petersburger, student of a theatrical school, knows the festival more from tasteless nonsense like 'The Hump-backed Horse' and artifacts in 'the Russian style' than from personal experience."[21] Years later, in his rather untrustworthy autobiography, Stravinsky also complained of Fokine's handling of the crowd scenes. "But it was a pity that the movements of the crowd had been neglected. I mean that they were left to the arbitrary improvisation of the performers instead of being choreographically regulated in accordance with the clearly defined exigencies of the music."[22]

For his part Fokine responded with a claim that the actions on stage were carefully choreographed to look chaotic. "Had I linked all the performers rhythmically to the orchestra and not allowed other rhythms and movements of the crowd then at one moment all would have had to become old men, at another—gypsies, at a third—drunks, at a fourth—bears. But I strove, and I had to strive, to make it look like everyone on the stage was living a varied, individual life . . ."[23] Still, the fact that, however well or badly he choreographed them, Fokine never entirely warmed to the crowd scenes in this ballet is clear from his complaints regarding the music: "The greatest difficulty for the artists in *Petrushka* is the final dance after the appearance of the mummers. It is in 5/8 time at a very fast tempo . . . Is this really necessary for the composer? I doubt it. I am sure that Stravinsky could have expressed the same wild dance in a rhythm more natural for that dance."[24] Such conflicts between the three main collaborators were inevitable but, as I have already noted, they did not result in creative paralysis. Instead, the final product incorporated each collaborator's concerns, producing the layering effect so characteristic of *Petrushka*. Thus, the context of the carnival was an important cultural source for Stravinsky and Benois (more so for the latter), while Fokine's emphasis was elsewhere.

In addition to the obvious connections to the general carnival scene mentioned above, a number of other specific points might well have influenced the final form of the ballet. Chief among these is the overall form of the typical plays produced in the balagany, wooden theaters capable of seating up to 1,500 spectators. They, like everything else connected to the carnival, were erected specially for it. Although various kinds of theatrical entertainments were presented, most of the shows went according to the following plan: "After a scene, constructed on 3–4 planes, in a luxurious setting with masses of participants, there would be a scene with just a few people for which a single plane would suffice . . . behind the scrim, during the performance of this scene, a new, richly decorated one would be prepared."[25] This, of course, describes the general outline of *Petrushka* quite nicely, for it, too, is composed of two richly decorated and multiplaned, well-populated scenes surrounding the more intimate and simpler scenes *à trois* that form the center of the ballet. What is more, the average length of a performance at the *balagany* was approximately forty minutes, the same length as *Petrushka*.

There is one other aspect of the Shrovetide carnival that played a crucial role in the formation of the libretto for *Petrushka*: the content of some of the plays that were performed inside the main wooden theaters. By the 1880s the repertoire consisted almost solely of bowdlerized dramatic versions of Russian classics and historical scenes. "From 1880, the onset of nationalism penetrated even into these theatres. . . . Frightful melodramas of national [pre-Peter the Great] history became popular; Pushkin and Lermontov came into fashion; the trend of entertainment was all towards morality and sobriety."[26] Stravinsky, who was born in 1882, could have seen and remembered only these dramas. Benois, on the other hand, who was born in 1870 and who possessed an excellent memory, recalled a very different type of show when he imagined the carnival:

> In the two chief *Balagani*, kept by Berg and Yegorev, Harlequinades were presented to the public. When I look back at my life, I consider it a remarkable stroke of luck that I had the opportunity of seeing these traditional pantomimes before they disappeared, for, thanks to them, Pantaloon, Pierrot, Harlequin and Columbine are, for me, not characters constructed by learned research into the *Commedia dell'Arte*, but real figures that I have seen with my own eyes.[27]

For Benois, these harlequinades became indelibly associated with the atmosphere of the carnival. It is not surprising then, that when given the opportunity to collaborate on a script set during Shrovetide, Benois endowed his characters with traits typical not for the puppet show that gave the ballet its name, but for the harlequinades he remembered so fondly. If we see Petrushka, the Moor, and the Ballerina as transformations of the *commedia dell'arte* figures Benois recalled from his childhood, we will go a long way toward understanding the sources for and the workings of the scenes involving the three main characters. This brings us to that peculiar realm where popular culture and the high literary tradition intermingle. For while the Petrushka puppet play belonged solely to the popular culture tradition, the *commedia dell'arte* (which had also begun as popular entertainment) had, by the early twentieth century, crossed into highbrow culture.

Petrushka and the Commedia dell'Arte Tradition

The *commedia dell'arte* was devised in sixteenth-century Italy where it quickly became a popular dramatic form. In the course of the next hundred years it spread throughout Europe, and its influence on drama and popular culture can be felt to the present day.[28] I, however, am not concerned with all the vicissitudes of its development. Instead, I concentrate on those of its transformations that played a role in the formation of the text of *Petrushka*. Broadly speaking, there are two such influences: the popular harlequinades that Benois knew as a child, and the renaissance that the *commedia dell'arte* enjoyed in high culture during the period of literary symbolism.

Benois, in his memoirs, recalls the harlequinades of the Russian *balagany* at carnival time:

> We see a village landscape, not at all Russian ... Old Cassandra is going to town and is giving instructions to his servants. One of them, dressed in white with his face covered in white flour, has a silly bewildered look ... The uneducated call him the miller, but I know that he is Pierrot .... But why is Harlequin wearing such a dirty shabby costume? ... Having started their work Pierrot and Harlequin begin to quarrel ... that clumsy lout of a Pierrot kills Harlequin ... it is then that the first miracle takes place. A fairy, brilliant with gold and precious stones, emerges from the hillock which has become transparent. She

approaches the folded corpse of Harlequin, touches it, and in one moment . . . Harlequin is alive once more; better still, after a second touch of the magic wand Harlequin's shabby attire falls off and he appears . . . in the guise of a handsome youth shining with spangles. . . . Cassandra's daughter, the adorable Columbine, comes running out of the house. The two are united by the fairy.[29]

This description covers only the first act, but we can already discern some points of similarity with the ballet. In the first place there is Pierrot's appearance, especially his "silly, bewildered look." This is the same clumsy, jerky Pierrot who, as Petrushka, will not be able to attract the Ballerina. The Harlequin, after his transformation, seems to be one of the ancestors of the handsome and sumptuously dressed Moor with whom the Ballerina (like Columbine in the pantomime) is in love. The connection is underscored by the fact that the Harlequin wore "a mysterious black half-mask."[30] It should be emphasized that in no case is a character in the ballet taken directly from these harlequinades. Only selected elements were used; these were combined with characteristics taken from other sources and synthesized either by Benois himself or, more probably, together with his collaborators who did not know the harlequinade tradition. Thus, although the harlequinade makes use of a fairy with a magic wand to bring the Harlequin to life, the Magician in *Petrushka* is but a distant relative of hers; his character is forged of many different sources most of them having nothing to do with her.

An example of how Stravinsky and Benois collaborated, and of the importance of the harlequinades for the latter, can be seen in their correspondence concerning the ballet's finale. When work was just beginning on the text, Stravinsky sent a letter to Benois in which he made the following comment: "It is my definite desire that «Petrushka» end with the magician on the stage. After the Moor kills Petrushka, the magician should come on stage and, having gathered up all three, that is Petrushka, the Moor, and the Ballerina, he should exit with an elegant and affected bow, the same way he exited the first time."[31] Benois, however, had his own ideas concerning the finale. In his conception it was not the Moor who kills Petrushka but the other way around, in the tradition of the pantomime of which he was so fond. When Diaghilev repeated Stravinsky's desire, Benois evidently felt compelled to go along. He was not happy about it though, as his petulant reply indicates: "The Moor kills Petrushka rather than

Petrushka the Moor. The last thing is not so important, though I prefer the image of Petrushka, tortured by jealousy and coquetry, finally breaking out and, as a result, freeing himself from the magician's depraved spells. But it's really not important."[32] In the end, Stravinsky's conception won out (although with serious modifications) and the murder and resurrection scheme typical for the harlequinades was not used. One might, however, detect a distant echo of this scheme in the resurrection of Petrushka's ghost at the ballet's conclusion. This was not in Stravinsky's original plan and it is possible that Benois's discussions of the harlequinade helped Stravinsky to resolve the problem of the finale, although, as we will see, there are plenty of other potential sources for the ending.

Petrushka and the Contemporary *Commedia dell'Arte*

More important even than the harlequinades for the development of *Petrushka* was the renaissance that the traditional *commedia dell'arte* figures underwent in the second half of the nineteenth century. The realists of midcentury had banished such conventionally artistic characters in favor of the drama of life. The symbolists, however, were attracted precisely by the conventionality of the three main figures (and particularly Pierrot). These recognizable characters could be infinitely stylized and used symbolically in a host of situations. It is by no means an exaggeration to note, as one scholar has, that:

> Pierrots were endemic everywhere in late 19th- [and] early 20th-century Europe as an archetype of the self-dramatizing artist, who presents to the world a stylized mask both to symbolize and veil artistic ferment, to distinguish the creative artist from the human being. Behind the all-enveloping traditional costume of white blouse, white trousers, and floured face, the Pierrot-character changed with the passage of time, from uncaring prankster to Romantic *malheureux* to Dandy, Decadent, and finally, into a brilliant, tormented figure submerged in a bizarre airless inner world.[33]

In Western Europe toward the end of the nineteenth century, Pierrot became the hero of poems, plays, and paintings. There was even a weekly satirical magazine that appeared in Paris from 1888 to 1891 under the title *Le Pierrot*.

It did not take the Russian symbolists long to recognize the potential inherent in the *commedia dell'arte* triangle. Aleksandr Blok seems to have been the first to pick up on it. He uses the three figures separately in a number of poems of the "Beautiful Lady" cycle but only once in his early poems does he put them together. After two stanzas that set a scene typical for the cycle (a ball that lasts all night), the poet tells us who the actors are:

Он встал и поднял взор совинный
И смотрит--пристальный--один
Куда за бледной Колумбиной
Бежал звенящий Арлекин.

А там--в углу--под образами
В толпе, мятущейся пестро,
Вращая детскими глазами
Дрожит обманутый Пъеро [34]

He rose and lifted up an owlish glance,
He looks – quite fixedly – alone,
Where after pallid Columbine
The jangling Harlequin has flown.

And there – aside – beneath the icons,
Within the colorful hurrying crowd,
With childlike eyes revolving,
Stands shaking, Pierrot, deceived.

This is not the place to analyze Blok's poetry, but it should be noted that there is a concern for the painful position of the Pierrot figure here, something that had been noticeably absent in the Russian versions of Harlequinades. Indeed, it is Pierrot, the childlike victim, the observer, the deceived one, who plays the central role in the poem.

An infinitely more developed variant of the same situation forms the basis for Blok's lyric drama *Balaganchik* (*The Fairground Booth*) of 1906. Meyerhold's production of this little play—in which he also starred as Pierrot—at the end of 1906 was of cardinal importance for *Petrushka*. Although there is no direct evidence that Benois, Stravinsky, or Fokine knew about the production (but in the close-knit Petersburg artistic world it is almost inconceivable that they did not), the figures of Blok and Meyerhold hover all around the edges of the ballet.[35] Aside from general theoretical similarities, there are a number of telling details. Thus, for example, Bely, describing the production of *The Fairground Booth*, says: "The characters only make typical gestures. If it's Pierrot then he sighs in only one way and flaps his arms in only one way."[36] Fokine, describing his thoughts on the choreography for *Petrushka*, says "But for the main characters I strove to create puppet-like, unnatural gestures."[37] This is evidently the same phenomenon described by Beaumont in his description of the ballet: "there was a curiously fitful quality in his (Nijinsky's) movements, his limbs spasmodically leapt or twisted or stamped."[38]

It was the production of *The Fairground Booth* that started Meyerhold thinking about the art of the grotesque. Although his theoretical writings on the subject were not published until 1912, he would have had ample opportunity to discuss them with Fokine and Benois in 1910 when all three were involved in a collaborative project. A number of Meyerhold's statements on the theater have obvious implications for the final form of *Petrushka*:

The fairground booth is eternal. Its heroes do not die; they simply change their aspects and assume new forms. The heroes of the ancient Atellanae, the foolish Maccus and the simple Pappus, were resurrected almost twenty centuries later in the figures of Arlecchino and Pantalone, the principle characters of the *commedia dell'arte*. . . . Banished from the contemporary theater, the principles of the fairground booth found a temporary refuge in the French cabarets, the German Überbrettl, the English music halls and the ubiquitous 'variétés.' If you read Ernst von Wolzogen's Überbrettl manifesto you will find that in essence it is an apologia for the principles of the fairground booth. . . . Wolzogen's manifesto contains an apologia for the favourite device of the fairground booth—*the grotesque*. . . . The grotesque mixes opposites, consciously creating harsh incongruity. . . . The grotesque need not necessarily be comic . . . it can as easily be tragic, as we know from the drawings of Goya, the horrific tales of Edgar Allen Poe, and above all, from E.T.A. Hoffman . . . the technique of the grotesque contains elements of the dance; only with the help of the dance is it possible to subordinate grotesque conceptions to a decorative task.[39]

These excerpts sound suspiciously like a program for numerous aspects of *Petrushka*. First of all, the reference to the special importance of the dance invites a balletic treatment of the fairground booth. The emphasis on the tragedy potentially inherent in the situation is important, as is the concern with the mixing of opposites. The mixture of the joyous revelry of the crowd with the tragic story of Petrushka, the Moor, and the Ballerina, the combination of the real and the fantastic, is precisely what gives the ballet its unsettling quality. The value of this combination of opposites was obviously important to Fokine, who characterizes his choreography for the main roles as "taken from life for the most inanimate puppet pantomime. Puppets' movements on a psychological foundation."[40] However, lest one think that Meyerhold's only influence on *Petrushka* was through an unpublished theoretical work, a glance at his theatrical activity in the period 1903–1910 provides grounds for rethinking. Throughout this period Meyerhold attempted to popularize the symbolist version of the *commedia dell'arte*.

He first played the role of Pierrot in 1903 in a play called *The Acrobats*, which he translated from the German of Frantz von Shentan. In the third act of that eminently forgettable work he appeared in a black clown's suit and whiteface as an aging, unsuccessful Pierrot. Then, in 1908, at a cabaret theater that he founded and that gave just one performance, Meyerhold staged a one-act play by P. P. Potemkin called, interestingly enough, *Petrushka*.[41] In October 1910, just before Benois and Stravinsky began work on the text of *Petrushka*, Meyerhold staged a version of a pantomime by Arthur Schnitzler entitled *Der Schleier der Pierrette* (Pierette's Veil—which for some reason was translated into Russian as *Sharf Kolombiny*, or Columbine's Scarf). In this rather gruesome version of the Pierrot story, Columbine is engaged to Harlequin. She decides to spend a last evening with Pierrot. He proposes a suicide pact and kills himself by taking poison. She runs away to her wedding ball but is haunted by the appearance of Pierrot's ghost. Terrified, she returns to Pierrot's room. When Harlequin finds her there, he becomes furious and locks her in with the dead Pierrot. She finally goes insane and drinks the rest of the poison. Throughout the production, music was provided by an orchestra led by a sinister conductor who, at the close of the play, was to run away from the scene in terror.

As was the case in the previously discussed Meyerhold connections, there are important links between *Columbine's Scarf* and *Petrushka*. The evil conductor seems related to the Magician who enslaves the puppets and brings them to life with his magic flute (although there are other sources for him as well). The Conductor's terrified flight at the end recalls that of the Magician when he sees Petrushka's ghost (here too there are other sources). Finally, the appearance of the ghostly Pierrot to scare a character (here Columbine and not the Magician) may have something to do with the vision of Petrushka's ghost at the end of the ballet. Indeed, the theme of Pierrot's ghostly resurrection is an invariant in all of Meyerhold's versions of the story.

Some smaller details also point up the importance of *Columbine's Scarf*. One relates to the question of how the traditional Harlequin became a Moor in the ballet. In Meyerhold's 1910 production of Calderon's *Adoration of the Cross*, the curtain was opened and closed by "two little liveried blackamoors."[42] The moor pops up again in the director's version of Schnitzler's pantomime. "*Columbine's Scarf* also saw the reappearance of the blackamoor proscenium servant. . . . On this occasion there was one only, who came on during the play to invite the audience to take refreshment."[43] Although there is no proof that Harlequin was transformed into the Moor under the influence of Meyerhold, it is certainly quite possible. In his memoirs Benois says he thought the Moor up himself (although this is clearly not true since Stravinsky's first letter to him, written before they had had any contact on the subject of the ballet, mentions the Moor), based on blackamoors who appeared during the intermezzos at some street performances of Petrushka plays. There are other possible sources as well, including the exotically dressed black slave who makes love to Zobeida in the ballet version of *Schéhérazade* that Benois wrote for Diaghilev in 1910. Again, it is important to remember that any or all of the subtexts mentioned above could have been relevant for a Russian audience, and that the ballet's aesthetic relies precisely on the tension generated by the recognition of multiplicity lying below *Petrushka*'s surface unity.

That Fokine was particularly affected by Meyerhold's ideas on the theater is not surprising considering that in 1910 he collaborated with the director on two projects. One, Gluck's *Orfeo* at the Mariinsky Theater, seems unimportant for *Petrushka*. The other, however, was a ballet called *Carnaval*, based on music by Schumann. The main characters were Harlequin, Pierrot, and Columbine. In his only ballet role, Meyerhold danced the part of Pierrot. Tamara Karsavina (the Ballerina for the first performances of *Petrushka*) was Columbine, and Nijinsky took the role of Harlequin. Although the plot of this little ballet is completely unrelated to that of *Petrushka*, one expects that the ever-alert Nijinsky and Fokine picked up on Meyerhold's experience with transformations of the *commedia dell'arte* and watched the way he played the "poor Pierrot, waving his long sleeves about."[44] The ballet was also important because it showed, in the words of Benois, "how close Fokine was to us and to our ideals."[45] It is easy to guess how easily the ethereal figures of Pierrot, Harlequin, and Columbine came to the minds of Fokine and Benois as soon as Diaghilev mentioned the ideas that he and Stravinsky had for a new ballet. Indeed, the text could have been created with such lightning speed only because much of its material was already part of the cultural vocabulary of the authors. Familiarity with the *commedia dell'arte* material, in various transformations, made it easier to come up with a new version.

As was the case with folk elements, the ballet's various authors were not equally receptive to symbolist poetry and to the Russian theater of the first decade of the twentieth century. Unquestionably, Benois was the most closely connected to symbolism. Its importance for Benois's thinking about the ballet can be seen from his *Reminiscences*, where, in discussing the personalities of the three main characters, he says: "If Petrouchka were to be taken as the personification of the spiritual and suffering side of humanity—*or shall we call it the poetical principle?*—his lady Columbine would be *the incarnation of the eternal feminine*; then the gorgeous Blackamoor would serve as the embodiment of everything senselessly attractive, powerfully masculine and undeservedly triumphant."[46]

The idea that Pierrot could be made to stand for the suffering artist or poet was a standard component of French symbolism; the elevation of Columbine to the level of the "eternal feminine" principle is, however, a particularly Russian phenomenon. In the decade or so before *Petrushka* the Russian symbolists had actively awaited the arrival of the incarnation of the feminine principle. This expectation is related to Vladimir Solov'ev's eschatological predictions of the appearance of "the woman clothed in the sun." Things went so far that, in 1904, Andrei Bely and Sergei Solov'ev decided that Blok's wife, Liubov' Dmitrievna, was actually the incarnation of the eternal feminine. They even posed for an absurd photograph together, flanking a table with the Bible and portraits of Vladimir Solov'ev and Liubov' Dmitrievna arrayed on it. In fact, triangular relationships like these that spilled from literature to life and back again played an important role in the cultural milieu of Russian symbolism.[47] Thus, the triangle of Blok, Liubov' Dmitrievna, and Bely in some sense led to *The Fairground Booth* and the triangle Bely, Nina Petrovskaia, and Valerii Briusov was fictionalized in the latter's novel *The Fiery Angel*. For Benois, who was closely acquainted with literary Petersburg, the ballet's triangle fit in quite nicely with the philosophical and literary mood of the epoch.

A consideration of the ballet's action in the context of Russian symbolism allows us one further interpretive possibility. Russian symbolist thought was characterized, in part, by strong millenarian leanings. Deriving their ideas from the philosophical and literary writings of Solov'ev, the Symbolists believed that they were living in apocalyptic times. Solov'ev's poem "Panmongolism" (1894) expresses in a compact way the central themes of the Russian symbolist apocalypse. The poem depicts the immanent end of the world caused by the eruption of dark, primitive, nomadic, pagan, and "Asian" forces, and their destruction of the political, religious, and cultural values of Western Europe. Dread in the face of these events is tempered, however, by a certain optimism, as the apocalypse would clear the ground for the appearance of a new and better civilization. For Solov'ev, the upcoming end of the world would be heralded by the appearance of Sophia, the incarnation of the eternal feminine. As apocalyptic prophecies multiplied, they became linked to a belief, probably derived from Dostoevsky, that Russian culture would provide the postmillennial civilization, for only Russia could mediate between Asiatic "barbarism" and European "rationalism."[48]

In the ballet, the Magician and the Moor are linked through their oriental features; as far as the Magician goes, recall the Asiatic turban on his portrait (discussed below in another context) as well as the stylized "oriental" music that appears in the second tableau when Petrushka looks up at the portrait. The Moor is not, strictly speaking, Asian, but he is emphatically not European and, as noted above, he calls to mind the exotically dressed black slave in the orientalist ballet version of *Schéhérazade*. Petrushka, on the other hand, is primarily linked with such European traditions as *commedia dell'arte* and its late nineteenth-century (primarily French) reincarnation. This opposition may help explain why the Magician appears constantly to egg the Moor on and to treat Petrushka in such a sadistic fashion. If we choose, then, we can see the ballet as an apocalyptic allegory in which the eternal feminine leads primitive Asian forces to destroy European culture. In this context, Petrushka's appearance over the fairground booth at the end of the ballet—in the person not of the effete European Pierrot but of the Russian Petrushka—would depict the ultimate triumph of Russian culture atop the ashes of both Europe and Asia.

If such symbolist interpretations were part of Stravinsky and Benois's plans, however, they seem largely to have been ignored by Fokine. As opposed to the first and last scenes in which Benois's concept of the carnival more or less prevailed, the inner tableaux were determined by the music and, especially, by Fokine's choreography and the artistry of the lead dancers. Fokine, it seems, had little use for symbolist theorizing on the nature of the main characters. His description of the Ballerina has nothing of the "eternal feminine" about it. "The Ballerina had to be a rather stupid, cute little doll."[49] Contemporary descriptions and photographs of the original production confirm that this was indeed the way Karsavina danced the role. As for Petrushka and the Moor, Fokine says: "The Moor is all 'en dehors,' Petrushka—'en dedans.' . . . The self-satisfied Moor is completely turned to the outside. Petrushka, unhappy, beaten and frightened, is all hunched up, he's retreated into himself."[50] This is hardly a symbolist-influenced interpretation.

If we can believe Nijinsky's wife, however, Nijinsky conceived his role neither in symbolist terms nor as a personal tragedy. She claims: "Vaslav amplified the crazy doll into the symbol of the spirit of the Russian people, oppressed by autocracy, but resurgent and unconquerable after all its abuse and frustration."[51] This potential dimension of the text does not seem to have been anticipated by any of the ballet's creators, a fact not surprising since the *World of Art* group and its successors were avowed foes of politically tendentious art. Still, it is possible that Nijinsky's personal conception of the role (which was, by all accounts, immensely powerful) was enriched by a "political" reading of *Petrushka*.[52] Such an interpretation of the ballet was not the only contemporary one that departed from the intentions of the libretto writers. The critic Cyril W. Beaumont (who said: "I have seen no one approach Nijinsky's rendering of Petrouchka, for . . . he suggested a puppet that sometimes aped a human being, whereas all the other interpreters conveyed a dancer imitating a puppet")[53] guessed that Nijinsky might have felt "a strange parallel between Petrouchka and himself, and the Showman [Magician] and Diaghilev." Such a suspicion cannot be merely dismissed considering the tumultuous relations between the two.[54]

We have now examined some of the connections between the ballet

Petrushka and European and Russian literary culture at the turn of the century. As was the case with the ballet's link to folklore, it turns out that, although the influences were many, they were never simply incorporated into the text. The fact of collaboration meant that each individual collaborator proposed ideas that were modified by his partners at various stages of the creative process. Due to the non-fixed nature of the text, such modifications could occur even in the moment of performance. It seems clear, however, that the crowd scenes in the first and fourth tableaux were more or less dependent on popular cultural sources, while the second and third tableaux reflect the influence of the literary tradition.

Petrushka and Nineteenth-Century Ballet, Opera, and Fiction

As it turns out, however, the two subtextual layers discussed previously are not completely adequate to explain the derivation of many small textual details and even some rather important moments in *Petrushka*. These can be understood only if we recognize the existence of still another field of expectations—this one evoked through allusions to and transformations of familiar (to the point of being clichéd) opera, ballet, and literary plots drawn from nineteenth-century sources. Each in his own way, Fokine, Benois, and Stravinsky were all closely connected to the artistic life of St. Petersburg and, therefore, knew the most popular operas and ballets almost by heart; it is thus not surprising that they borrowed from some of them. As a rule, however, their borrowing was of a very specific type.

In discussing their use of these sources it will be helpful to keep in mind the idea of parody, as defined by Iurii Tynianov. Tynianov claims that parody is one way for an author to come to terms with the works of an overly powerful predecessor. "Stylization is close to parody. Both of them live a double life: Beyond the plane of a work is a second plane, a stylized or parodied one. But in parody there is an obligatory discrepancy between the two planes, a dislocation; the parody of a tragedy will be a comedy . . . the parody of a comedy could be a tragedy."[55] This is precisely how the writers of *Petrushka* seem to have come to terms with some of the most popular and well-known themes of nineteenth-century ballet. The most obvious case concerns the theme of the doll's coming to life or, more generally, the animation of nonanimate figures.

Since its first production in 1870, *Coppélia* has been a staple of the ballet repertoire. It entered the repertory of the Imperial Ballet in 1884, and was certainly familiar to the creators of *Petrushka*. Indeed, the ballet was a favorite of Benois's, who wrote: "I am sure that my artistic development was immensely influenced . . . by the ballet Coppelia."[56] At the center of the story is the doll *Coppelia*, the lifelike creation of the toymaker Coppelius. Indeed, she is so lifelike that young Frantz falls in love with her. The ballet contains two scenes of animation: In one, a group of village girls led by Frantz's former fiancée Swanilda set various mechanical toys in motion; in the other, Swanilda takes the place of Coppelia, and, after Coppelius pronounces various spells she "comes to life," creates havoc amongst Coppelius's mechanical toys, and steals back her fiancé. The end of the ballet shows the lovers united, ready to live happily ever after.

The elements of *Coppélia* parodied in *Petrushka* are quite obvious. In the former, a character with a soul pretends to be a doll. In the latter, three dolls take on human form. The bumbling Coppelius is replaced by the truly sinister Magician. Finally, the comic ending of *Coppélia*, in which the lovers are united, is reversed in the tragic rejection of Petrushka by the Ballerina and in Petrushka's death. Even small details of *Coppélia* are reproduced and inverted in *Petrushka*. For example, after she has magically come to life, one of Swanilda's mischievous acts is to pick up a sword, with which she stabs the figure of a Moor (one of Coppelius's mechanical toys). In the finale of *Petrushka* it is the Moor who kills Petrushka with a sword. *Coppélia* was itself a romanticized (parodic in its own way) adaptation of a story by E.T.A. Hoffmann called "The Sandman." It is not impossible to see *Petrushka* as a sort of return to the original text, although only in spirit—for there do not seem to be any details in the ballet that would suggest the original. In the story, Coppelius is a sinister figure and the ending is not one of lovers united but of Frantz's insane suicide. This tie to Hoffmann is all the more plausible because he was one of the authors constantly cited by Meyerhold as crucial for the concept of the grotesque.

Coppélia is by no means the only popular nineteenth-century ballet based on material from Hoffmann to include animated dolls. Another such work is the most popular ballet chestnut of them all: Tchaikovsky's *The Nutcracker*. In that ballet, the mysterious Drosselmeyer brings a trio of toys (consisting of a toy soldier, Columbine, and Harlequin) to life. Nor are animated dolls unique to ballets based on stories by Hoffmann. A ballet called *Fairy Doll* was presented a number of times in Petersburg in the first decade of the twentieth century. A contemporary reviewer of the first performances said: "The whole interest of the piece lies in the successful imitation of living people through the movements of automatized figures."[57] As if any more potential sources were necessary, the ballet includes a *pas de trois* for the Doll and two Pierrots. Fokine himself danced one of the Pierrots in the 1903 production at the Mariinsky. That production was not lost on Benois either, who had good things to say about it in his *Reminiscences of the Russian Ballet*. Benois and Fokine even used a variation of this same theme themselves in the first ballet on which they collaborated for the Ballets Russes. In *Le Pavillion d'Armide*, a tapestry comes to life and, in a prefiguration of themes from *Petrushka*, the boundaries between the real and created worlds are blurred.

Thus, the theme of the doll or puppet coming to life, absent from both popular cultural and symbolist treatments of Pierrot, seems to be a transformation of a popular convention of nineteenth-century ballet. In those ballets, however, it was always clear to the spectator that dolls were dolls and people were people. The transformation from one world to another was effected by trickery (*Coppélia*) or dreams (*The Nutcracker*), or the entire ballet was simply set in a magic world (*The Fairy Doll*). What is unique about *Petrushka* is the thoroughgoing ambiguity of its situation. The overlap between the "real world" of the carnival and the created world of the puppets is not explicable by recourse to sleight of hand or dreams. The tragedy of Pierrot cannot be dismissed as a fairy tale because the puppets are simply too human.

Familiar ballets were not the only potential source of high-cultural plot material; operas played a role as well. Discussing his early influences, Stravinsky says: "I remember having heard another lyrical work that same winter, but it was by a composer of the second rank—Alexander Serov—and on that occasion I was impressed only by the dramatic action. My father had the leading part, a role in which he was particularly admired by the Petersburg public."[58] Although Stravinsky does not name the opera, he is undoubtedly referring to Serov's *The Power of the Fiend*. Stravinsky's father was known for his portrayal of Eromka, a character who "stood for the dark forces at large within the world of man."[59] There is even a self-portrait of Stravinsky's father in this role.

The opera takes place during the Shrovetide carnival in seventeenth-century Moscow, and the fourth act puts a naturalistic version of the carnival on stage. Eromka's most famous aria is called "*Shirokaia maslenitsa*"

(Shrovetide in Full Swing). In the autograph orchestral score of *Petrushka*, this was the title that Stravinsky gave to the fourth tableau[60] (it was changed to "Folk Revelry at Shrovetide" in all published editions). In addition, Taruskin has found direct musical evidence of connections between *The Power of the Fiend* and *Petrushka*. On the level of text, however, no such direct connections can be made. The opera may well have provided certain general thematic ideas but, as we have seen, there were a number of competing sources available, including Stravinsky's and Benois' own happy memories of the carnival. The relationship of the ballet to the opera is, at best, one of transformation. In the opera the wild and disturbing carnival scene corresponds to the turmoil in the inner lives of the characters; there is something evil inherent in the carnival itself. In the ballet, on the other hand, the troubled psyche of Petrushka and his tragic fate stand in stark contrast to the generally joyous and innocent fun of the carnival. The relationship of Eromka to the Devil is clearly metaphoric, but the source of the "magic" in the ballet is ambiguous, and not wholly explicable in human terms.[61]

The concepts of magic and the forces of evil lead us to take a closer look at another figure whose role cannot be explained merely by referring to popular culture or symbolism. While it is true that there were charlatans who performed various magic tricks in some of the small *balagany*, the role of the Magician in *Petrushka* is far more important than that of the simple street charlatan. It should be remembered that the Magician possesses several attributes linking him to infernal forces. In the first place, the special curtain that rises and falls between the tableaux shows the Magician enthroned in the sky. A second version showed a group of demons floating over Petersburg. Secondly, it is the sound of his magic flute that brings the puppets to life. Finally, a malevolent portrait of the Magician stares down at Petrushka from the wall of his room and reminds him of the imprisonment of his soul in a puppet's body.

The theme of the sorcerer who imprisons men (but more usually women) in nonhuman bodies was common enough in nineteenth-century ballet. The most famous version is Tchaikovsky's *Swan Lake*, in which an evil magician, Von Rotbart, holds Odette prisoner in the form of a swan. Only the manly Siegfried's bravery can break the enchantment and allow her to resume her shape as a woman. In addition to recalling ballets like *Swan Lake*, however, the connection of the Magician to the Devil links *Petrushka* to a much more important and powerful Russian literary tradition.[62]

It is a strong possibility that the Magician's infernal traits, and a number of other details in the ballet, derive from the works of Gogol. In her discussion of the ballet, Krasovskaia mentions a possible connection to the story "Nevsky Prospect," but she does not provide any details. In addition to "Nevsky Prospect," at least two other stories by Gogol are important for the ballet: "The Portrait" and "The Overcoat." In "The Portrait" a young artist, Chartkov, uncovers an unusual portrait in a Petersburg junk shop. It is that of an older man of Southern extraction draped in an Asiatic costume. Chartkov buys the portrait and, with the help of the money that he finds in the portrait's frame, becomes a fashionable and highly successful portrait painter. Gradually, however, it becomes clear both to the reader and to Chartkov that the subject of the portrait was an infernal incarnation and that in accepting the money and fame it brought the artist has, in fact, sold his soul to the Devil. Chartkov tries to escape from the influence of the portrait but its power is too strong. Finally he goes insane.

The idea of the portrait/devil was not unique to Gogol's story (it is also the conceit of Oscar Wilde's *The Picture of Dorian Gray* [1891], for example) but Benois, who knew the Russian classics extremely well, probably had Gogol in mind while painting the Magician's portrait. As he describes it: "According to my plan, this portrait was to play an important part in the drama: the conjurer [Magician] had hung it there so that it should constantly remind Petrouchka that he was in his master's power."[63] The portrait itself, as can be judged by a later version, shows an old, dark-skinned man, full face, in a vaguely Asiatic turban. Once again, however, this Gogol connection seems to have been made only by Benois. In fact, most of the supernatural and demonic motifs in the ballet can be attributed to him. When the portrait was damaged in transit before the premiere, Bakst made another on short notice. The new one, which evidently satisfied Diaghilev, Stravinsky, and Fokine, showed the Magician in profile, a circumstance that would have weakened the Gogol connection considerably. When Benois arrived in Paris and saw the new portrait, he created a major scandal, resigning as Diaghilev's Artistic Director.

Withal, the most interesting Gogolian touch in *Petrushka* concerns the finale. Here, the connection was evidently made only by Stravinsky and not by his collaborators. In a conversation with Robert Craft, Stravinsky says: "The resurrection of Petroushka's ghost was my idea not Benois'. I had conceived of the music in two keys in the second tableau as

Petroushka's insult to the public, and I wanted the dialogue for trumpets in two keys at the end to show that his ghost is still insulting the public."[64] Unfortunately for Stravinsky, however, Fokine was in charge of realizing ideas in dance and he clearly did not see the finale the same way. Later Stravinsky complained: "Fokine's choreography was ambiguous at the most important moment. Petroushka's ghost, as I conceived the story, is the real Petroushka, and his appearance at the end makes the Petroushka of the play a mere doll. . . . The significance of this . . . is not and never was clear in Fokine's staging."[65] Since Fokine's concern was primarily on the humanness of Petrushka, which is hidden under his doll's skin, it was inevitable that his and Stravinsky's conceptions should clash. Nevertheless, despite varying interpretations, Petrushka did appear over the top of the little theater at the end of the ballet and he did make a threatening gesture at the Magician/Devil that scared the latter out of his wits.

The reviewer for *Apollon* almost made the proper literary connection when he said: "one might cavil with the excess psychologism of the final moment (the resurrection of the murdered Petrushka as a hint of the existence of a 'double')."[66] The actual connection to Russian literature is not, however, through the tradition of the double; rather, it is through the theme of the downtrodden little man and, particularly, Gogol's story "The Overcoat," which began that tradition. In the story, an insignificant civil servant, Akaky Akakievich, scrimps to acquire a new overcoat. After a series of misadventures this coat is stolen. When he goes to lodge a complaint, the bureaucracy, incarnated in *an important personage* (a character who has been perceived as the Devil in several interpretations) snubs him and Akaky dies of a fever induced by walking improperly clad in a Petersburg winter. What interests us about the story is its conclusion. Rumors begin to circulate in Petersburg that a ghost has appeared who looks like a civil servant. One of Akaky Akakievich's fellow clerks recognizes him and the ghost "threatened him with his finger." Finally, the ghost appears to *an important personage,* the man directly responsible for Akaky's death and symbolically equivalent to the entire bureaucratic system that kept Akaky subhuman and enslaved. "The poor *important personage* practically died" from this vision. In the ballet, of course, Petrushka, the downtrodden, half-human puppet, comes back to haunt the evil Magician.[67]

As with all of the other textual parallels discussed previously, the connection here is not direct. Literary subtexts merely provided a series of themes that could be borrowed, reversed, or transformed, or that could be used to suggest levels of meaning present in the ballet but not necessarily fully developed. Sometimes the relation between *Petrushka* and earlier texts appears to be polemical. More frequently, however, the authors reused old and clichéd material in new dramatic contexts. Audiences did not necessarily have to connect such moments with their high-cultural sources. In this case, for example, it is equally plausible to connect the resurrected Petrushka to the endings of the "Petrushka" plays. These, as has been noted previously, usually finished with Petrushka being dragged off to hell. But since the showman had to motivate the next performance (as is normal for street theater, such performances were more or less continuous), he frequently ended with a promise of the main character's resurrection.[68] Thus, the same moment could be perceived as at once a distant echo of Gogol's story, a reinterpretation of the traditional ending of the popular Petrushka play, or an uneasy mixture of both simultaneously.

Petrushka and Russian Theater

Turning from the ballet's sources to the libretto itself, we can say that, through the complex intertextual play that resulted from its heterogeneous sources the finished product echoed a number of the central concerns of contemporary Russian theater. Primarily, these had to do with two inter-related concepts: The call for a more imaginative use of theatrical space, and a heightened interest in the spectator—in particular, a desire to break down traditional audience expectations. As has been noted by Lynn Garafola, Diaghilev's Russian collaborators were all aware of the advances that had been made by Stanislavsky and Nemirovich-Danchenko's Moscow Art Theatre starting as early as 1898. They were also aware of the sharp critiques, both theoretical and practical, that had been leveled at Stanislavsky's methods by adepts of Russian symbolism as well as by Stanislavsky's erstwhile student Meyerhold. As usual, *Petrushka* represents a blend of the theatrical theories and practices characteristic of these seemingly incompatible schools. According to Garafola, Fokine's staging of the ballet, and indeed his entire choreographic orientation, was marked by a Stanislavskian concern with theatrical naturalism.[69] At the same time, the frames in which this naturalism operated were provided not by Fokine himself but by Benois, who was far more interested in the then avant-garde theories and practices of symbolism (though he nevertheless admired the

Moscow Art Theatre). If we examine more closely the theatrical frame of the ballet, we can see that its concerns were those of Stanislavsky's critics rather than those of the Moscow Art Theatre.

In the final version of the ballet the action occurs on at least three different levels. The first is the street where the carnival is in full swing. The little theater of the Magician fronts onto this street but when he opens the curtain of his theater to reveal the three puppets, the audience becomes, as it were, doubled. That is, the characters who had been wandering about the stage become spectators of the puppets' dance. The theater audience watches them watch the dance and it watches the dance as well. The result is that the audience is watching two ballets simultaneously. The doubling of the fourth wall causes it to disappear, and unsettles spectators' expectations about their relationship to the onstage action. This all may sound quite antinaturalist, even avant-garde, but as is frequently the case with *Petrushka*, this modernist effect could equally well have been derived from a low-cultural source. In his memoirs, Benois describes his childhood vantage point for performances of puppet shows: "We sat, as in a box, on the window sill, while below the caretakers, handymen and shopkeepers arrived. . . . Sometimes the crowd around the screen roared with the kind of laughter provoked by dirty jokes, and on such occasions my brothers threw conspiratorial glances at each other and Mamma looked anxious."[70] Thus, Benois and his family were in the position of the theater audience in the first tableau of *Petrushka*. Not only did they watch the puppet show, but they also watched the real-life reactions of certain spectators. The modernist theatrical concerns of the first tableau had a prior existence in Benois's experience. As was the case with individual sections of the text, the staging could have been read either in the context of popular culture or in that of contemporary theatrical concerns. The meaning of this gesture is, of course, completely different depending on which set of interpretive assumptions the spectator brings. If one chose to see *Petrushka* in the context of the Russian carnival, this doubling was an example of theatrical mimesis. If, on the contrary, one looked at it in the context of contemporary Russian theater, the same scene served as a modernist attempt to break down theatrical mimesis. The ideal spectator would have recognized both possibilities simultaneously, and would have appreciated the ballet as a complicated play with both sets of concerns.

The question of how spectators were supposed to conceptualize this scene as a whole is further complicated by the fact that while at this point in the ballet the audience is meant to perceive the crowd on stage as "real" people and the solo dancers as animated puppets, the actual effect in the theater is inevitably just the reverse. The "puppet" roles are always taken by the company's famous lead dancers; their names are in the program and their faces are recognizable even under the theatrical makeup. This was particularly true of the original production; Nijinsky and Karsavina were celebrities, known to the entire ballet-going public. The corps dancers, on the other hand, are generally unknown, and the audience tends to see them as a faceless and not entirely human crowd. Thus, the spectators' perceptions are pulled in two opposite directions. They know the principle dancers as people but are asked to perceive them as animated dolls, while they see the corps de ballet as glorified dolls but, in the context of the ballet, they must see them as real people.

The second and third tableaux work in many respects to call into question the conclusions to which the audience has been led in the first tableau. Theoretically, these tableaux take place far backstage. That is to say, the theater audience is transported behind the wings of the Magician's theater to see what the on-stage audience does not see: the private drama of Petrushka, the Moor, and the Ballerina. The fact that the audience for these two tableaux was not exactly the same as for the first caused Stravinsky some problems. On 2 February 1911, Stravinsky told his collaborator that he had decided: "to eliminate the drum roll before Petrushka (second tableau) and before the Moor (third tableau)." His reasoning was that "the drum roll is meant to invite the listeners on stage, that is the carnival crowd, to the spectacle. It is not the audience sitting in the theater in Monte Carlo or Paris. . . . Petrushka's scene as well as that of the Moor are not meant for the carnival crowd but for us. Therefore, the drum roll is out of place here. Isn't it?"[71] In fact, Stravinsky was absolutely correct. The drumrolls here do cause a confusion between the different planes on which the action of the ballet takes place. Benois, however (who was always more eager to employ modernist theatrical devices than was Stravinsky), evidently wanted a certain amount of confusion on this point, and he eventually prevailed upon Stravinsky to retain the drumrolls.

The change in perspective from the first to the second and third tableaux throws into high relief the ways in which the libretto manipulates the audience's fields of expectation. If the expectations evoked by the first tableau are primarily connected with the carnival, the Petrushka play in its folk incarnation, naturalist theater, distance (as emphasized by placing the audience at double remove from the action), and comedy, then the second and third tableaux evoke unmistakably the symbolist lyrical chamber drama, intimacy, and tragedy. But what makes juxtaposition such an effective theatrical device is that the new expectations introduced by the second and third tableaux do not and cannot eliminate the expectations that had been evoked in the first tableau. Instead, these seemingly incompatible theatrical perspectives coexist and amplify one another.

The fourth tableau does not so much resolve this conflict as sharpen it. The expectational fields, which had heretofore been segregated, are put on stage simultaneously in the finale. Thus, the fourth tableau begins on the same level as the first but here, unexpectedly, the hierarchy that had been carefully preserved to this point breaks down. First of all, both the audience on stage and the theater audience hear cries from behind the closed curtain of the theater. Then Petrushka, the Moor, and the Ballerina come out of their segregation and intermingle with the "real" world. In the first tableau, they danced among the revelers as puppets, but now the human qualities with which they were seen to be endowed when they were backstage turn out to coexist with their puppet status, at least momentarily. The tension is temporarily dissipated by the appearance of the Magician, but the appearance of Petrushka's ghost (or the real Petrushka) adds the final ambiguous touch.

If we are to believe Stravinsky's memoirs, the series of interlocking perspectival planes was originally intended to be even more complicated. He claims: "another of my ideas was that Petroushka should watch the dances of the Fourth Tableau (the Coachmen, the Nurses, etc.) from a hole in his cell and that we, the audience, should see them, too, from the perspective of his cell."[72] Had this plan been adopted it would have created a neat reversal of the first tableau in which the theater audience watches the on-stage audience watch the puppets, and would have further confused audience expectations about theatrical mimesis.

Nevertheless, even the less-complicated staging that was ultimately adopted served to blur the borders between watcher and watched, human and puppet, to create a stylized theatrical experience—one that, in keeping with the theatrical culture of the time, called into question the kind of naturalism that had been pioneered in the Russian theater by Stanislavsky. While the first tableau was presented as arch-realism, the second and third could clearly not be "read" realistically. Finally, by combining the realistic and fantastic worlds in the finale, the authors called the very distinction between the stage world and the real world into question. By blurring the expected boundaries of audience and actors, the final product succeeded in creating the illusion for which Benois had lobbied in his second draft letter to Stravinsky: "The apogee is a finale group dance with crashing and ringing. We have to do it so that the whole theater dances along."[73]

The end result was captured best by Benois himself: "*Petrushka* lasts just 3/4 of an hour, but, as if by a conjuring trick, not only does a single man's life pass by in that time, but so does the tragedy of the collision of the life of one with the life of everyone."[74] It was the uneasy relationship between reality and irreality that Benois saw as the unique feature of *Petrushka*. "The doubled psychology of the ballet confused many; both those who wished to solve some kind of worn-out symbolic riddles in it and those who came to see a ballet like *The Rose* [*Le Spectre de la Rose*]."[75] The first, it would seem, are those who wished to see a completely nonmimetic work, while the second type hoped for a return to an easily comprehensible romantic balletic never-never land. In any case, *Petrushka* lives up to the theatrical ideals of Benois who, in his regular newspaper column, informed Nikolai Evreinov that theater "can only be a «captivating deceit» if one believes that external deceit is covering up some kind of truth."[76]

The authors were not, of course, without precedent in their attempts to break down audience expectations of mimetic theater in the name of a higher truth. Meyerhold had shown the way in his theoretical articles and in his pathbreaking production of Blok's "lyrical drama," *The Fairground Booth*. In fact, in regard to the relationship of audience to actors, *Petrushka* looks at times like an answer to Meyerhold's theoretical demand that the theater "lower the stage to the level of the orchestra, and, having built the diction and the motions of the actors around rhythm, bring closer the possibility of the rebirth of dance."[77] The director's description of the situation on stage at the beginning of his 1905 staging of Blok's play illustrates the similarities between his conception and that adopted by Benois: "The whole stage is hung at the sides and rear with blue cloth; this expanse of blue serves as a background and it sets off the color of the set of *the little theater erected on the stage. The little theater has its own stage, curtain, prompter's box* . . ."[78] In fact, compared with the avant-garde theatricality of Blok's lyrical drama, the text of *Petrushka* seems positively old hat. For ballet, however, which was usually peopled by magical figures with no connection to the real world and, therefore, could never jar the audience's expectations of reality, such a text was new. In addition, the combination of hyperrealism at the beginning of the first tableau with the emphatically nonmimetic portions of the rest of the ballet would have been unusual even for the more advanced dramatic theater.

But the aspect of *Petrushka* that best illustrated the ballet's close connection to contemporary theater was the ambiguous balance it struck between the puppetlike and human characteristics of the characters. It was evidently Benois who first sensed the importance of blurring the line between puppet and human. He returns to this problem again and again in the drafts of his letters to Stravinsky: "The effect will be bigger if we give enough *time* to let the puppets 'live through' their dream, *to let them for a moment really become living people.* The Ballerina would jump out of Petrushka's booth for the last time in *real* (already not in puppet) terror."[79]

That the theater of the future would include puppet actors in some form or another was one of the givens of Symbolist dramatic theory. Most of the contributors to the 1908 collection *Theater: A Book About the New Theater*, devoted to the theater of the future mentioned this topic. For some, most notably Meyerhold, the appearance of the puppet-actor was a positive development. Such an actor would subordinate himself to the director's conception of the play. Thus, in discussing Maeterlinck, Meyerhold is happy to assert that "his tragedies demand radical immovability, practically marionette-like (*tragédie pour théâtre marionette*)."[80] The system of acting that Meyerhold was to develop in the 1920s, with its emphasis on biomechanics, exemplifies the control that the great director wished to have over every aspect of an actor's performance. Although Meyerhold's ideal eventually led to some spectacular theatrical productions, the call for actors to become puppets threatened implicitly to dehumanize the theater.

Most symbolist writers, including some of the contributors to the 1908 book, found the implications of Meyerhold's theory at least somewhat disturbing. Valerii Briusov, for one, argued for some kind of middle ground because he feared that "for the ultimate triumph of 'stylized' theater only one thing is left: to replace actors with puppets on strings carrying gramophones inside . . . there is no doubt that the modern 'stylized' theater is taking the straightest road to marionette theater. But the more consistent a 'stylized' production will be, the more it will coincide with mechanical theater, the less it will be necessary."[81] It was, however, Fedor Sologub who subjected the theories of "stylized" theater to the most withering scorn. In his contribution to this same volume, he asked in a sarcastic tone: "And why, by the way, should an actor not be a marionette? This shouldn't offend anyone. The immutable law of universal play states that a person is like a wonderfully constructed marionette."[82] Then, Sologub launches into an allegorical tirade that, on closer examination, sounds amazingly like a preliminary proposal for the finale of *Petrushka*:

> And there, lying on a cloth awaiting its final bathing, lies a puppet, worn out and needed by no one, its arms folded as someone has folded them, its legs stretched as someone has stretched them, its eyes closed as someone has closed them—a poor marionette good only for a tragic play! From out there, from the wings, someone indifferent jerked you on an invisible cord, someone cruel tormented you with the fiery torture of suffering . . . and out here, in the orchestra your clumsy movements amused somebody."[83]

The difference between this anguished description and the ballet's finale is mostly that Benois and Stravinsky reinterpreted the whole plan in a positive artistic light. "Suddenly the magician appears. He pushes apart the crowd, . . . leans over the victim and . . . lifts up a *puppet*-Moor from whom, with a smile, he extracts a cardboard knife. Then he goes to Petrushka's booth, opens it with a little key, and pulls out a puppet, a stupid idiotic Petrushka puppet. The same thing happens next with the Ballerina."[84]

Thus, although the central role played by puppets links the ballet with contemporary theatrical theorizing, *Petrushka*, with its insistence on showing the presence of a human soul inside the puppet's body, represents an important development—a juxtaposition, that humanizes Meyerhold's theorizing by taking the Symbolists' apprehensions into account. The extent to which Sologub's fears turned out to be unjustified (at least in this instance) can be seen in Ia. Tugenkhol'd's review of the first production in *Apollon*: "the performers (Nijinsky, Orlov, and Karsavina) were so imbued with the seriousness of this '*puppet*' drama that they were able not only to *amuse* the spectator through the strangeness of their 'cardboard' rhythms, but to force him to sympathize with the romantic *tragedy* of Petrushka-Pierrot."[85]

Conclusion

The success of the *Petrushka* text, which was patched together, as we have seen, from an amazing number of sources and grew from the often contradictory impulses of three nonprofessional writers, can best be measured from a review of the first American performance: "This piece, with all its exaggerated grotesquerie and burlesque features in the music—music that would be wholly unintelligible, useless and tedious apart from each single detail of the accompanying action—evidently made a deep impression on the public—an impression of amusement and exhilaration." [86]

By combining and layering three separate groups of sources, all of which were part of the contemporary cultural stock of Russian audiences, the authors of *Petrushka* created a Russian *Gesamtkunstwerk* that was both true to the ideals of modernist theater and tremendously effective on stage. *Petrushka* fulfilled the Russian theatrical ideal of the early twentieth century—an ideal that was expressed in productions which, in the words of one who was intimate with Diaghilev's circle, "demanded of all who took part in them the same mood, enthusiasm, and general understanding in which they were created." [87]

NOTES

1. For a more complete treatment of the ballet in all its collaborative glory, see A. Wachtel, *Petrushka: Sources and Contexts* (1998), from which this chapter has been adapted.
2. Taruskin, 1996, vol 1, chap. 10, pp. 661–778.
3. Stravinsky, p. 49.
4. Benois, 1941, p. 324.
5. Ibid., p. 325.
6. Olearius, p. 142.
7. Kelly, 1990, pp. 49–54.
8. For a detailed review of various versions of the *Petrushka* play see Kelly, 1988. See also Nekrylova, especially pp. 76–93. The latter book also contains some excellent illustrations.
9. This passage appears in the drafts for *Diary of a Writer*. See Dostoevsky, 22:180.
10. Kelly, 1990, p. 62.
11. See A. Wachtel, 1998, p. 125.
12. Ibid., p. 135.
13. Alekseev-Iakovlev, p. 47.
14. Benois, *Rech'*, 17 August 1911.
15. Benois, 1968, p. 182.

16. Stravinsky and Craft, *Expositions and Developments*, p. 32.
17. Both of the articles from which these passages are taken are quoted in Leifert, pp. 61 and 63. The latter description, by the way, sounds very much like Gogol's description of a crowded Nevsky Prospect in his story of that name.
18. From letter to Benois of 3 November 1910. See A. Wachtel, 1998, p. 125.
19. This comes from the rough draft of a letter from Benois to Stravinsky dated 9 December 1910. See A. Wachtel, 1998, pp. 126–127.
20. Benois, 1964, 1:119.
21. Benois, *Rech'*, 17 August 1911. *The Hump-Backed Horse* is a popular ballet in five acts to a libretto by Arthur Saint-Leon with music by Cesare Pugni. The ballet, based on the fairy tale of Peter Pavlovich Ershov, premiered in St. Petersburg in 1864.
22. Stravinsky, 1936, p. 35.
23. Fokine, 1961, p. 284.
24. Ibid., p. 283.
25. Leifert, p. 34.
26. Benois, 1964, 1:128.
27. Benois, 1941, p. 30.
28. For an excellent and exhaustive treatment of the *commedia dell'arte* in twentieth-century culture see Green and Swan.
29. Benois, 1964, 1:125–126.
30. Benois, 1941, p. 35.
31. From letter of 3 November 1910. See A. Wachtel, 1998, pp. 124–125.
32. From draft letter of Benois to Stravinsky. See A. Wachtel, 1998, pp. 126–127.
33. Youens, p. 96.
34. Aleksandr Blok, 1955, pp. 99–100. Translation mine.
35. For an extensive discussion of this problem, see Ritter, pp. 181–187.
36. Quoted in Meyerhold, 1968, 1:250.
37. Fokine, 1961, p. 286.
38. Beaumont, 1940, p. 44.
39. Meyerhold, 1968, 1:222–229.
40. Fokine, 1961, p. 287.
41. I have been unable to find anything out about the content of this play. Its low quality, however, can perhaps be inferred from a contemporary review which termed the work "without content and nauseatingly insipid." Quoted in N. Volkov, 2:38.
42. Meyerhold, 1969, p. 112.
43. Ibid., p. 114.
44. Auslander, pp. 35–36.
45. Benois, 1941, p. 319.
46. Benois, 1941, 1:326, emphasis mine.
47. For more on the theory and practice of love triangles among the Russian symbolists, see Olga Matich, "The Symbolist Meaning of Love," in Paperno and Grossman, pp. 44–50, and Irina Paperno, "Pushkin v zhizni cheloveka Serebrianogo veka," in Gasparov, et al., pp. 24–27. See also the discussion of this phenomenon in the previous chapter devoted to Blok's play *The Unknown Woman*.
48. Dostoevsky expressed his belief in Russia's messianic role frequently in his *Diary of a Writer*.

49. Fokine, 1961, p. 287.

50. Ibid., p. 287.

51. Nijinsky, p. 107.

52. The fact that Nijinsky did indeed play a role in the construction of at least his own character seems certain. This is what Benois had to say on the subject in an interview: At the first rehearsals "Nijinsky exécutait, mesure après mesure, d'après les données de Fokine et du musicien. A ce moment-la il avait plûtot l'aspect d'une poupée. Il obéissait aux directive reçues. Mais à la première répétition en costume il s'est transfiguré. Il a animé le personnage triste, tragique, sans aucunement le souligner par un maquillage comme on l'a trop fait depuis. Son goût personnel lui permettait de saisir ces subtiles nuances (. . .) Il a ciselé ce rôle d'une façon extraordinaire et, en ce sens, on peut lui en attribuer la paternité." Quoted in Reiss, p. 67.

53. Beaumont, 1940, p. 45.

54. Green and Swan bring this interpretation to the fore in their discussion of *Petrushka*. See pp. 67–68.

55. Tynianov, p. 416. Although this view may seem similar to views held by Harold Bloom and other Freudian critics, it differs in that Tynianov's Russian writers tend to cite and thereby incorporate their predecessors rather than attempt to kill them.

56. Benois, 1964, 1:138.

57. Quoted in Krasovskaia, p. 77. This ballet was originally staged in Vienna in 1888 as *Die Puppenfee*. It was restaged at the Mariinsky Theater by Nikolas and Sergei Legat (designed by Bakst) in 1903.

58. Stravinsky, p. 6.

59. Taruskin, 1981, p. 165. For more on this interpretive possibility, see Farkas.

60. A microfilm copy of this score (which belongs to M. Fokine's son's widow) can be found in the New York Public Library's Dance Collection. The score is signed Igor Stravinsky and dated Rome, 13/26 May 1911.

61. Another opera that appears to have played a significant source role for *Petrushka* was Leoncavallo's *Il Pagliacci*. See Ritter, p. 214, for a thorough discussion of this subtext.

62. It should also be noted that the occult in general and magic in particular exercised an enormous hold over the Russian imagination in this period and had done so for some time. Indeed, Tolstoy had already satirized the Russian fascination with spiritualism in 1889 in his play *The Fruits of Enlightenment*. Nevertheless, most of the Russian symbolists, including Briusov and Bely were inveterate followers of the occult. For more on this, see Maria Carlson. There is no direct indication, however, that esoteric subjects were of particular interest to any of the *Petrushka* collaborators.

63. Benois, 1941, pp. 333–334.

64. Stravinsky and Craft, *Expositions and Developments*, p. 137.

65. Stravinsky and Craft, *Memories and Commentaries*, p. 34.

66. Tugenkhol'd, p. 74.

67. The possible connection between this scene and Gogol's story is noted as well in Kelly, 1990, p. 103.

68. Ibid., p. 96.

69. Garafola, pp. 19–25.

70. Benois, 1964, 1:114.

71. Letter from Stravinsky to Benois. A. Wachtel, 1998, p. 134.

72. Stravinsky and Craft, *Memories and Commentaries*, p. 34.

73. See A. Wachtel, 1998, pp. 124–138.

74. Benois, *Rech'*, 17 August 1911.

75. Benois, *Rech'*, 17 August 1911.

76. Benois, *Rech'*, 15 February 1913.

77. Meyerhold, "*Teatr. (K istorii i tekhnike)*," in *Teatr. Kniga o novom teatre*, p. 175.

78. Ibid., p. 250, emphasis mine.

79. See A. Wachtel, 1998, pp. 124–138.

80. Meyerhold, "*Teatr. (K istorii i tekhnike)*," *Teatr. Kniga o novom teatre*, p. 152.

81. V. Briusov, "Realizm i uslovnost' na stsene," in *Teatr. Kniga o novom teatre*, p. 253. In a separate article published in the same year, Blok also expressed fear and dismay at the "dictatorship of the director." ("O teatre," *Zolotoe runo*, no. 3–5, 1908.)

82. F. Sologub, "Teatr odnoi voli," in *Teatr. Kniga o novom teatre*, p. 188.

83. Ibid., pp. 188–189.

84. Rough draft of letter from Benois to Stravinsky. See A. Wachtel, 1998, p. 126.

85. Tugenkhol'd, p. 74, emphasis mine.

86. Unsigned review of the U.S. premiere of *Petrushka*, *The New York Times*, 25 January 1916, p. 10.

87. Dobuzhinsky, p. 402.

CHAPTER 5

The Adventures of a Leskov Story in Soviet Russia, or the Socialist Realist Opera that Wasn't

THE BROAD QUESTION TO BE CONSIDERED in this chapter is how authors, works, or even whole traditions of one period are assimilated into the culture of another, particularly after moments of cataclysmic change. I am concerned here with the reception of nineteenth-century Russian literature by early Soviet culture, but the general problem is by no means confined to Russia in the twentieth century.[1] To adduce only one example, in fourth-century Rome after conversion to Christianity a generation that had been educated according to the best principles of pagan rhetoric and literature had to reconceive their previous cultural canon in a new ideological context. One method they chose was the cento, a patchwork literary genre that, in its most celebrated exemplar, used nothing but whole poetic lines taken out of context from the works of Virgil in order to retell the stories of the Old and New Testaments.[2]

By the late 1920s, members of the Soviet creative intelligentsia found themselves in an analogous position. They were heirs to a vigorous literary tradition, one they knew practically by heart and could not easily jettison, yet the ideological changes introduced in the wake of the Bolshevik revolution ensured that the nineteenth-century canon could not be folded unproblematically into the new culture. To be sure, some urged the wholesale abandonment of prerevolutionary Russian culture, but the advocates of a complete purge of the "steamship of modernity" were in the minority and eventually lost out. Instead, in tandem with the development of Soviet culture, a slow process of assimilation and, necessarily, reinterpretation of the classics began. In the case of some authors, the process went fairly smoothly, either because, like Nikolai Chernyshevsky, they had been on the right side (or, more accurately, the left) in the Tsarist days, or because, like Tolstoy, they had received the stamp of approval from on high. On the

This essay was inspired by Hugh McLean's article "The Adventures of an English Comedy in Eighteenth-Century Russia: Dodsley's *Toy Shop* and Lukin's *Scepetil'nik*." A shorter version was published in Simon Karlinsky, James Rice, and Barry Scherr, eds., *O Rus! Studia litteraria slavica in honorem Hugh McLean*. (Berkeley, CA: Berkeley Slavic Specialties, 1995), pp. 358–368.

other end of the spectrum were writers like Konstantin Leontiev, whose religious and aesthetic views were simply incompatible with those of the Soviet state and who could not be assimilated at all. For most nineteenth-century writers, however, the situation was not clear-cut. Active mediation was needed, either by critics who could contextualize the work of an author in terms needed for acceptance, or by writers and artists who could revise, borrow from, adapt, or otherwise integrate a given work.

Nikolai Leskov was one of those nineteenth-century figures who did not easily fit into the new interpretive schema. For one thing, his political qualifications were decidedly questionable: he had written novels vilifying the left (*No Way Out*, 1864, and *At Daggers Drawn*, 1870–71). And although in later years he had mostly avoided politics, his extravagant writing style and fondness for folk religion did not endear him to those who would soon come to see writers as "engineers of human souls." The problematic nature of Leskov for Soviet culture is reflected in postrevolutionary publishing history and criticism. According to Hugh McLean's authoritative study, the first collected edition of Leskov in the Soviet period did not appear until 1956–58, and "apart from a few scattered articles, no new full-length study of Leskov was published until 1945."[3] But if the Soviet publishing industry and the critics were uninterested in packaging Leskov for the new culture (with the exception of a few innocent tales like "Lefty"), the same cannot be said of Soviet artists. Their efforts to Sovietize Leskov are the focus of my discussion here. In particular, I will concentrate on the adventures of a single Leskov story, "Lady Macbeth of the Mtsensk District" in the artistic maelstrom of the first decades of Soviet culture.[4]

"Lady Macbeth" is by no means a typical Leskov story. It describes how the wife of a provincial merchant (Katerina Lvovna Izmailova), in concert with her lover (Sergei), murders her father-in-law, her husband, and her nephew. The murders are discovered, however, and she and Sergei are sentenced to Siberian exile. On the way there, enraged by Sergei's unfaithfulness, Katerina hurls both his new lover and herself to death by drowning. This tale does not employ the *skaz* narrator present in most of Leskov's more famous works, nor at first glance does it foreground the peasant, folkloric aspects of Russian culture.[5] On the other hand, it makes a fine candidate for transposition into other genres, adaptation, or stylization, because it is itself a transposition—a Russification of Shakespeare's tragedy. As such it is by no means unique in Russian nineteenth-century realism, joining Ivan Turgenev's "Hamlet of Shchigrov District" and "King Lear of the Steppes" among others.[6]

Remaking Leskov's story into a work that would be acceptable within the artistic canons of incipient Socialist Realism was the intent of the 23-year-old composer Dmitrii Shostakovich when he began work on his opera *Lady Macbeth of Mtsensk* in 1930.[7] This becomes apparent as soon as we read the statements he made concerning the piece in the early 1930s. For example, in the program book that accompanied the first production Shostakovich claimed that "no work of Russian literature . . . more vividly or expressively characterizes the position of women in the old pre-revolutionary times than Leskov's." But, he continued, "Leskov, as a brilliant representative of pre-revolutionary literature, could not correctly interpret the events that unfold in his story."[8] Statements of this kind were standard fare in the rehabilitation of classic Russian writers. As the message of the story in question could not be approved, it was imperative to attribute that message to the ideological constraints of the author's time, constraints against which he was seen to have been struggling. This method could be called Soviet deconstructionist criticism, and its initiator was the great deconstructor himself—Lenin, in his influential articles on Tolstoy.

Shostakovich, however, felt it necessary to do more than explicate those moments of Leskov's story that could be seen as "politically correct" in 1930. In order to be elevated from the merely acceptable into the pantheon of classics, Leskov's story needed further interpretation. It had to be understood as a harbinger of the most progressive trends; it had to contain positive elements, as opposed to being merely an implicit criticism of its own time. Shostakovich found these positive elements through a clever reinterpretation, or more accurately, a revision of the main character, Katerina Izmailova. According to the composer: "N. Leskov depicts the main heroine of his story . . . as a demonic figure. He finds no reasons either for a moral or even a psychological justification of her. . . . I interpreted Katerina Lvovna as an energetic, talented, beautiful woman, who is destroyed by the gloomy, cruel, family surroundings of serf-owning-merchant Russia." Katerina is thus transformed from a voluptuously lustful and crazed murderess into a victim of nineteenth-century society, while her lover Sergei is dubbed "a future kulak." Leskov's story is lauded as "a depiction of one of the gloomiest epochs of pre-revolutionary Russia," a hymn to the "suffering people of that epoch—an epoch built on the humiliation of the exploited by the exploiters."[9] The loaded words

Shostakovich employs to describe the world depicted by Leskov betray the kind of anachronistic and revisionist thinking about history that was typical among the Soviet creative intelligentsia.

It is the revision of Katerina, however, that reveals Shostakovich's basic sympathy for the thrust of early Socialist Realist art, particularly its obsession with the creation of a positive hero.[10] As Shostakovich put it: "My task was to justify Ekaterina Lvovna in every way possible so that that the listener and viewer would be left with the impression that she is a positive character." This was, as the composer was aware, a tall order. As he noted immediately, "it is not very easy to elicit sympathy: Ekaterina Lvovna commits a series of acts which are not in accord with morals or ethics—two murders."[11] Here, of course, anyone who has read Leskov's story recognizes that one way in which the composer tries to rehabilitate Katerina is by eliminating the third, most disturbing murder in the story— that of her young nephew and co-heir Fedor Liamkin—a murder that cannot be explained away by reference to the cruel domination of patriarchal Russia.

Shostakovich's attempt to rehabilitate Katerina was not confined to omitting uncomfortable material. He used the full range of resources available to an operatic composer. Indeed, as Richard Taruskin observes, the effort to raise Katerina to the level of heroine is even more pronounced in the music than in the libretto: "Evoking a wealth of familiar musical genres and invoking a bewilderingly eclectic range of styles, the composer makes sure that only one character is perceived by the audience as a human being. From the very first pages of the score, Katerina's music is rhapsodic, soaring, and—most telling of all—endowed with the lyric into-nations of Russian folk song. . . . In total contrast, every other member of the cast is portrayed as sub-human."[12] Katerina's lyrical laments separate her from the more dissonant vocal lines of the other characters, drawing a sharp boundary between positive and negative figures.

Furthermore, there is evidence that, had Shostakovich's plans not been interrupted, Katerina would have come to be seen as still more heroic through her association with a trio of further operas devoted to the "position of women in Russia." In a 1934 interview Shostakovich said:

> I want to write a Soviet "Ring of the Nibelungen." This will be an operatic tetralogy in which "Lady Macbeth" will be a kind of "Rheingold." The main image of the following opera will be a heroine

of the "People's Will" Movement. Then a woman of our century. And finally, I will describe our Soviet heroine who combines in herself the qualities of the women of today and tomorrow, from Larissa Reisner to the best concrete pourer at the *Dneprostroi* Zhenia Romanko.[13]

Katerina would thus have become a progenitor of female heroism, and Shostakovich's operatic reinterpretation of Leskov would have placed both the twentieth-century composer and the nineteenth-century author firmly within the Socialist Realist canon.

The question then arises, If Shostakovich composed an opera that was meant to be a politically correct statement and if he did so in keeping with what would be the main lines of Socialist Realist aesthetics, why did his opera fail (ideologically speaking, that is)? For fail it certainly did, and in the most spectacular of fashions. The story of the disaster has been told frequently. *Lady Macbeth* premiered practically simultaneously in Leningrad and Moscow in January 1934. It ran for almost two years, until Stalin went to a performance in early 1936. Unfortunately for Shostakovich, the Soviet leader and arbiter of good taste hated the work, which was banned almost immediately afterward. The new attitude toward *Lady Macbeth* was expressed in a notorious *Pravda* editorial entitled "Muddle Instead of Music":[14] "The music croaks and hoots and snorts and pants in order to represent love scenes as naturally as possible. And 'love' in its most vulgar form is daubed all over the opera. The merchant's double bed is the central point on the stage. . . . The author uses all the means at his disposal to attract the sympathy of the spectators for the coarse and vulgar aims of the merchant's wife, Katerina Izmailova."[15]

The problem, as the above excerpt makes clear, was that Shostakovich failed to realize that overt eroticism was no longer acceptable in the Soviet arts. All his efforts at creating a model Soviet opera foundered on the explicit sexuality that was, first and foremost, a property of the music, although it was evident in the staging and the libretto as well. Interestingly enough, in this area, too, Shostakovich took considerable liberties with his source text, for Leskov's story, while built around Katerina's passion, is nowhere near as blatantly sexual as Shostakovich's transposition. Various theses have been advanced to account for the increased eroticism of Shostakovich's opera, but to appreciate fully the reasons behind his foregrounding of sexuality we need to know how Shostakovich became interested in the story. Furthermore, an excursus into the origins of

Shostakovich's interest in the story may also help us to understand why the young composer chose Leskov to rehabilitate; for given Leskov's absence from the Soviet pantheon this was hardly inevitable. Shostakovich's opera was not, in fact, the first Soviet-era transposition of "Lady Macbeth." Indeed, it is my contention that the operatic transposition was made not directly from Leskov, but rather from an intermediary version dating from the early 1920s that comes from a surprising source: not literature or music but rather visual art. Moreover, the transposition in question introduced an entirely new cultural layer to Leskov's nineteenth-century realism, one of high modernist culture in its Russian incarnation.

In 1919–20, the celebrated artist Boris Kustodiev painted a series of "Russian types."[16] When he contracted with the publishing house Akvilon to issue them in book form, they asked the young writer Evgenii Zamiatin to contribute an accompanying text. The result was the story "Rus'," published together with the drawings in 1922.[17] This collaboration is unusual, particularly because it represents a rare example of a writer working in response to illustrations rather than the other way around. For our purposes, however, it is more important to note on the one hand the erotic nature of some of Kustodiev's drawings, and on the other the links between Zamiatin's text and Leskov's "Lady Macbeth of Mtsensk." The former is clearest in a picture entitled *A Beauty* (*Krasavitsa*, 1915, fig. 5–1), which depicts a voluptuous, bare-breasted woman with the same face as Kustodiev's other merchant's wives, though it is a general feature of many of Kustodiev's paintings featuring merchant-class women (fig. 5–2).

"Rus'" is a minor masterpiece, a tour de force that incorporates most of the types depicted in Kustodiev's drawings into a narrative derived from Leskov's "Lady Macbeth." The story concerns a young, well-endowed (in all senses of the word) orphan, Marfa, who is encouraged by her aunt to choose a husband from among the rich merchants in her provincial town. She marries Vakhrameev, an older man who treats her well, but who is clearly unable to satisfy her desires. The story hints that she takes a lover, probably from among her husband's employees. One day her husband dies: "after dinner he lay himself down to sleep—and he never got up. It seems that the cook had fed him some toadstools at dinner together with the morels, that's what did him in, supposedly. Others said something different—well, what don't people say."[18] Finally, Marfa remarries (her young lover, evidently), but, in contrast to Leskov's, this story ends happily.

Fig. 5–1.
B. M. Kustodiev,
A Beauty (*Krasavitsa*),
1915.

Fig. 5–2.
B. M. Kustodiev, *Au Bain*
(*V bane*) ("Vénus russe"), 1915.

A wealth of circumstantial evidence leads to the conclusion that the connection between Leskov's story and Zamiatin's is not, as at least one critic believes, merely coincidental.[19] First, it is well known that Zamiatin was a great admirer of Leskov. In particular, one might recall his wildly spectacular "people's theater" piece *The Flea* (1925), a loose adaptation of Leskov's story "Lefty." The sets and costumes for that work's Leningrad and Moscow productions were, by the way, executed by Kustodiev.[20]

Fig. 5 3.
Title page from the 1930 edition of
N. S. Leskov's *Lady Macbeth of Mtsensk
District* (design executed in 1923).

Fig. 5–4.
Kustodiev's illustration
from the 1930 edition of
N. S. Leskov's *Lady Macbeth
of Mtsensk District*
(design executed in 1923).

More important, in both of these stories folkloric material is used in the same way: not on the level of language, but rather as a structuring element in the narrative.[21] Further evidence that "Rus'" and "Lady Macbeth" were related, at least in Kustodiev's eyes, can be found by comparing his drawings of "Russian types" with the illustrations he produced in 1923 for an edition of "Lady Macbeth" (see fig. 5–3).[22] The latter drawings, like the previous set, are in many cases unabashedly erotic (figs. 5–4 to 5–8). But the most compelling evidence is the drawing that accompanies the opening of chapter 1, which is nothing more than a revision of the first drawing in the book edition of "Rus'" (see figs. 5-9, 5-10).

Figs. 5–5 through 5–7.
Kustodiev's illustrations
from the 1930 edition
of N. S. Leskov's *Lady
Macbeth of Mtsensk District*
(designs executed in 1923).

Fig. 5–5

Fig. 5–6

Fig. 5–7

Fig. 5–8.
Kustodiev's illustration
from the 1930 edition of
N. S. Leskov's *Lady Macbeth*
of Mtsensk District
(design executed in 1923).

Fig. 5–9.
Katherine Izmailova, from
Kustodiev's illustrations
to the 1930 edition of
Leskov's *Lady Macbeth*
of Mtsensk District
(design executed in 1923).

Fig. 5–10.
Untitled depiction of a
merchant's wife, from
B. M. Kustodiev's collaborative
1923 work with E. I. Zamiatin,
Rus: Russian Types.

But what does this sequence of visual art works have to do with Shostakovich and his opera? After all, the Soviet Union in the mid-1930s was worlds apart culturally from that of the early 1920s. It turns out, however, that although Shostakovich should have been far too young to have been actively aware of the cultural climate of the immediate post-revolutionary years (he was born in September 1906), he had been a frequent visitor in the Kustodiev household as early as 1919, when as a child prodigy he had been asked by his schoolmate, Irina Kustodieva, to play for her wheelchair-bound father. Kustodiev took a liking to the young pianist and his family, who even spent part of the summer of 1923 at the painter's Crimean dacha. At the time Kustodiev was working to complete his illustrations for "Lady Macbeth."

In *Testimony*, Solomon Volkov records the following remarks of Shostakovich concerning Kustodiev:

> I was deeply impressed by Kustodiev's passion for voluptuous women. Kustodiev's painting is thoroughly erotic, something that is not discussed nowadays. Kustodiev made no secret of it. He did blatantly erotic illustrations for one of Zamiatin's books. If you dig deeper into my operas *The Nose* and *Lady Macbeth*, you can find the Kustodiev influence in that sense. Actually, I had never thought about it, but recently in conversation I remembered a few things. For instance, Leskov's story "Lady Macbeth of Mtsensk District" was illustrated by Kustodiev, and I looked through the drawings at the time I decided to write the opera.[23]

At this point it might be of interest to see, in turn, the origins of Kustodiev's voluptuous women, for this was his main legacy to the young Shostakovich. Although Kustodiev could hardly be called the most avant-garde of early twentieth-century Russian artists, his Russian beauty had an excellent modernist pedigree. Her immediate predecessor can be found in two works from 1912 by Mikhail Larionov. The first, quite realistic for Larionov, depicts a voluptuous—although somewhat awkward and grotesque—woman lying on a bed in practically the same position as Kustodiev's "Beauty." (see fig. 5–11). By her feet is a large red cat, a detail absent from Kustodiev's *Venus* painting but present in his illustrations for "Lady Macbeth." While Kustodiev's woman is clearly meant to tempt the male gaze, it is not clear whether the woman in Larionov's painting has

Fig. 5–11.
M. F. Larionov,
"Katsap Venus," 1912.

Fig. 5–12.
M. F. Larionov,
Venus (Venera), 1912.

any sexual allure to speak of. The other painting, more typical of Larionov's naif work of this period, has the word "Venera" (Venus) written boldly on the painting and depicts a highly stylized woman oriented in a similar fashion to Kustodiev's (fig. 5–12) The vase with a single flower echoes the floral wallpaper and painted bedframe in Kustodiev's work. Tracing the origins of these works, in turn, we can guess that the Larionov paintings are Russified versions of an original French work that itself marked a melding of modern French art with a primitive, and to European eyes, highly erotic culture. I have in mind Paul Gauguin's 1896 canvas *Te arii vahine* (fig. 5–13). This painting now hangs in Moscow's Pushkin Museum, which means that it was in Sergei Shchukin's private collection in Moscow and would have been known to Larionov. What we can deduce

Fig. 5–13.
Paul Gauguin,
Te arii vahine
(The King's Wife),
1896).

from this progression is that Larionov borrowed from Gauguin's work, simultaneously further primitivizing and rendering grotesque his exotic South Sea beauty. Kustodiev domesticated Larionov's work, making his Venus incontestably Russian and undoubtedly sexually tempting.

With all of this information at our disposal, we can now trace the path that Leskov's story traveled on its way toward Shostakovich's opera. In our reconstruction, the initial impulse was provided by Zamiatin, who fashioned "Rus'" as an adaptation of Leskov's "Lady Macbeth." Kustodiev evidently recognized the underlying plot connection, and this probably inclined him to illustrate "Lady Macbeth" in 1923. In his mind, the temptress Katerina was connected to the archetype of the Russian beauty, the primitive Venus as she had been portrayed by Larionov and before him by Gauguin. The young Shostakovich did not, then, come to Leskov by accident, but rather through the mediation of Kustodiev, who gets credit for the hypersexualization of Leskov's tale.[24] By the time Shostakovich began work on the opera he may well have forgotten the intermediate steps, but they remained present in the heightened eroticism of the opera, the very thing that got the composer in trouble despite all his conscious efforts at remaking Leskov's story for the Socialist Realist canon. Thus, although most critics have seen Shostakovich's work as a transposition of Leskov's story, it was in fact a double transposition. The intermediate layer, provided by high modernist culture, proved decisive for its ultimate failure as a Socialist Realist work despite the composer's intentions. By the mid-1930s, sex in public was unacceptable. So while it might have been possible to bring Leskov's story into the Soviet canon in the mid 1930s, it proved impossible to do so for a Lady Macbeth seen through the mediation of Kustodiev and Larionov.

The case of Shostakovich's opera forces us to recognize that, in at least some cases, it is incorrect to assume that the connection between a classic work and a later reinterpretation or adaptation is direct. Rather, such rehabilitations tend to occur within an accumulative and semicontinuous process. A new interpretation is often mediated by and to some extent dependent on previous reinterpretations, and it may even be the case that an intermediate transposition can have a decisive impact on what a newer version looks like, sometimes despite the desires of an author. That was certainly the case with *Lady Macbeth*, as the mediation of Russian modernism interfered with Shostakovich's desire to recanonize a classic work.

From our standpoint at the beginning of the twenty-first century, however, it is of little concern whether Leskov and his story succeeded in entering the Soviet canon in the 1930s. Rather, the fact that Shostakovich's opera has endured long after most of the cultural productions of this period have been forgotten illustrates that the most powerful artworks created in the Soviet Union in the 1930s are by artists who were trying to work within the system yet who were unable to do so successfully; to Shostakovich's opera we can add such works as Kazimir Malevich's faceless peasant paintings from 1928 to 1932, and Andrei Platonov's *Kotlovan*.[25] In each of these cases, we find a productive tension when cultural paradigms typical of Russian high modernism collided with those of incipient Socialist Realism. Unlike the destructive collision of matter and antimatter, however, this interaction of seemingly opposite forces was at times capable of generating genuine works of art.

NOTES

1. In this essay early Soviet culture means Soviet culture, beginning in the late 1920s. The period from immediately after the Revolution until the late 1920s was one of artistic ferment and general tolerance (although many individuals and groups were, of course, highly intolerant). It was not until the late 1920s that a state-approved Soviet culture began clearly to emerge.
2. For an excellent discussion of this phenomenon, see Jeffrey Schnapp, "Reading Lessons: Augustine, Proba, and the Christian *Détournement* of Antiquity," SLR 9.2 (1992): pp. 99–124.
3. McLean, p. 749.

4. For a general catalogue of versions of "Lady Macbeth" in Soviet culture of this period see, L. Anninskii, *Leskovskoe ozherel'e* (Moscow, 1986), pp. 70–108.

5. As Faith Wigzell puts it, "from the Formalists onwards Leskov's language, particularly in its contribution to an obviously stylized narrative texture has undergone a reevaluation. Critical attention, as a consequence, has tended to be directed towards the works with the most colourful *skaz*, at the expense of those works which do not possess a so obviously stylized narrative texture, such as *Ledi Makbet Mtsenskogo uezda*" (p. 169). Wigzell goes on to show quite convincingly that folkloric elements are present in the story, albeit on different and more subtle levels.

6. According to Hugh McLean: "The point of such titles is to juxtapose a Shakespearean archetype at a high level of psychological universalization with a specific, local, utterly Russian, and contemporary milieu. The effect on a Russian reader of that time was almost oxymoronic: how could there be a Lady Macbeth, especially nowadays, in such a mudhole as Mtsensk?" (McLean, p. 146).

7. In discussing the transposition of a short story into an opera, we must be careful not to automatically ascribe all changes to differences in genre: some have to do with medium, as Caryl Emerson notes. See her *Boris Godunov: Transpositions of a Russian Theme*, pp. 4–8. In this case, however, we will see that the changes to Leskov's story were the result of generic or ideological choices rather than medium constraints.

   Clearly, I reject Ian MacDonald's assertion that the opera "can reasonably be interpreted as a deliberate, if necessarily disguised, expression of antagonism to Communism" (*The New Shostakovich* [Boston, 1990], p. 93). This claim, which is based primarily on the most dubious sections of *Testimony*, flies in the face of everything Shostakovich said about his own opera, and even if one believes that he was consciously or unconsciously coerced into the statements I quote here, that is belied by the extent to which the work adheres to the basic patterns of incipient Socialist Realist art.

8. Quoted in Taruskin, 1988, p. 29.

9. All quotations here are taken from the unpaginated introduction to Shostakovich, *Sobranie sochinenii v sorok dvukh tomakh*, vol. 20 (1985).

10. For more on the search for a positive hero at this time, see Régine Robin, *Socialist Realism: An Impossible Aesthetic*, trans. Catherine Porter (Stanford, CA: Stanford University Press, 1992), pp. 217–296.

11. Shostakovich, vol. 20, unpaginated introduction.

12. Taruskin, 1988, p. 31.

13. Shostakovich, vol. 20, unpaginated introduction.

14. For a blow-by-blow account of the cultural situation in the Soviet Union surrounding the *Pravda* editorial, see Leonid Maksimenkov, *Sumbur vmesto muzyki: Stalinskaia kul'turnaia revoliutsiia, 1936–1938* (Moscow, 1997), pp. 72–112.

15. Quoted in Taruskin, 1988, p. 33.

16. For reproductions of some of the watercolors, see M. G. Etkind, ed., 1982, pp. 177, 179, 181, 183, and 189.

17. *Rus'. Russkie tipy B. M. Kustodieva, slovo Evg. Zamiatina* (Petersburg: Akvilon, 1923).

18. "*Rus'*," in Zamiatin, 2:51.
19. Leonore Scheffler minimizes the possible connections between the two works. "Das Motiv der Pilzvergiftung, das der Autor ohne Hinweis auf ursächliche Zusammenhänge und Hintergründe hier einfach als Tatsache mitteilt, hat gelegentlich an Leskovs Ledi Makbet Mcenskogo uezda erinnert. Zieht man Leskovs Erzählung ingesamt zum Vergleich heran, dann wird zugleich deutlich, wie andersartig Zamjatin das Thema der Leidenschaft behandelt." *Evgenij Zamjatin: Sein Weltbild und seine literarische Thematik* (Köln, 1984), p. 238.
20. See Etkind, (1982), pp. 301, 302, 309, 310, and 312–313 for reproductions of sketches for the sets and costumes for this production.
21. For more on this, see Wigzell for Leskov and for Zamiatin see Thomas R. Beyer, "Rus': A Modern Russian Folk Tale," *Russian Language Journal* (1986): pp. 107–113.
22. For reasons I have not been able to discover, the edition of "Lady Macbeth" that contained these drawings was not actually published until 1930.
23. Volkov, pp. 8–19. Serious questions have been raised concerning the truthfulness of Volkov's book. See the critique by Laurel Fay, "Shostakovich versus Volkov: Whose *Testimony*?" *Russian Review* vol. 39 no. 4 (1980): pp. 484–493. There is little doubt, however, that the book is based on conversations between the two men. Most of the questions have to do with Volkov's attempt to present Shostakovich as a dissident rather than with the content of discussions such as this. In any case, it is unlikely that Volkov could have invented this particular conversation as it would have required knowledge about the composer's early years that would not have been easily available except from Shostakovich himself.
24. Alternatively, Shostakovich might have been reminded of the "Lady Macbeth"/Kustodiev connection by Zamiatin, for the two worked together when Zamiatin wrote one scene for Shostakovich's previous opera, *The Nose*.
25. For a treatment of these other works in this context, see A. Wachtel, 1999.

CHAPTER 6
The Theatrical Life of Murdered Children

EVEN BEFORE THE START of Aleksandr Vvedensky's 1938 play *Elka u Ivanovykh* (*The Ivanovs' Christmas Party*), the reader is presented with an extremely puzzling list of dramatis personae that includes some seven "children or merely devils" ranging in age from infancy to 82 years. While the play cannot be said to present an entirely coherent action, among the central events that occur in the course of its four acts, set in the 1890s, are the murder of one of these children by her nanny, the nanny's subsequent arrest, and then, in the final scene, the death of all the "children" as well as the parents.

As is typical for the dramatic work of the OBERIUTY, the motivations of the characters are not very clear.[1] That a specter of death hovers over the Puzerov house, in which most of the play takes place (there are, by the way, no characters named Ivanov in the play despite the title), is, however, clear from the very beginning. The first line of the play, spoken by the one-year-old Petia Perov is: "Will there be a Christmas party [*elka*]? There will. But suppose there won't. Suppose I were to up and die."[2] The first actual death in the play takes place before the end of the opening scene. Sonia Ostrova (a "little girl" of 32) threatens to expose herself when the Christmas tree is lighted, provoking a rebuke from the Nanny. When Sonia then insults the Nanny she "grabs an ax and cuts off her [Sonia's] head," saying, "you deserved this death" (p. 158). When the police arrive to discover the headless corpse they ask what happened and the children tell them that the nanny is guilty. When they inquire as to the whereabouts of the murderer, she replies: "I stand before you. Tie me up. Lie [*sic*] me down. And punish me" (p. 159). The nanny, however, is not always prepared to accept responsibility for her actions, and at a number of junctures in the play she claims to be insane.

A good portion of the remainder of the play is concerned with the nanny's fiancé, the woodcutter Fedor (considered by Milivoe Iovanovich to be an evocation of Dostoevsky).[3] Fedor's main interest appears to be sex, and when the nanny's arrest eliminates her as a sexual partner he instead has sex with a maid in scene 6. The quantity of deaths begins to multiply in scene 8, which occurs on Christmas day. That is, in the logic of this play, the holiday that is supposed to commemorate a mystical birth turns into its opposite, a festival of death. As the nanny is to be led into the courtroom, the first judge says, "Not having made it until Christmas, I have died" (p. 169). He is then replaced by a second judge, who also dies immediately. Despite these unexplained deaths, another judge is found who pronounces the nanny guilty and sentences her to death. The final, ninth scene of the play returns us to the Puzyrev house where, despite the death of Sonia, the Christmas party is to take place. The party, however, is marred first by the suicide of Volodia Komarov (a boy of 25), and then in immediate succession by the deaths of all the remaining children and, finally, of the mother and father.

The consensus among scholars who have attempted to make sense of Vvedensky's "absurd" work, is that the play is a parody. There is not, however, much agreement regarding what the object of such a parody might be. Thus, B. Müller considers it a parody of a tragedy, though he does not provide a specific source. Alice Stone-Nakhimovsky does not consider literary parody but rather describes the work as a "social parody" against bourgeois morals of the end of the nineteenth century. Milivoe Iovanovich, on the contrary, finds exclusively literary subtexts, ingeniously noting connections between Vvedensky's play and Dostoevsky's work, in particular *Crime and Punishment* and *Notes from the House of the Dead*.[4] Finally, Graham Roberts focuses on Vvedensky's work not as a parodic commentary on any genre or specific set of texts, but rather as a critique of mimetic theater in general: "in this play Vvedensky foregrounds the process of aesthetic reception, and specifically the addressee-oriented nature of drama. Moreover, Vvedensky thereby questions the Aristotelian notion of drama as mimesis, a notion which united Naturalist, Symbolist, and (Socialist) Realist dramatic models."[5]

Each of these interpretations has merit. However, with the exception of Roberts's, the various subtextual analyses fail to provide any overall interpretive paradigm. They do not ask why Vvedensky would have wanted to write a parody (regardless of the source text or texts) at this time and in this form. But surely this must be a central question. Why, for example, would Vvedensky have cared in 1938 about bourgeois society of the 1890s? Why would he have felt the need at this point to engage the form of literary tragedy given the tragic reality of Soviet society in this period? And why would Fedor Dostoevsky in particular have been on his mind? In my view there is not much point in digging up subtexts unless one can use them to provide an interpretative framework for a given literary work. Thus, in considering the intertextual background of Vvedensky's play in this chapter, I will specifically concern myself with explaining not merely the literary subtexts found in the text but some of the reasons why Vvedensky might have been interested in them. In so doing, I will be following the lead of Roberts, but, as opposed to him, I think it important to recognize the specific subtextual material used in the play. For if one does not do so, it is hard to see what differentiates this play from any other OBERIU dramatic text, particularly from Daniil Kharms's *Elizaveta Bam* which clearly attempts to unseat Aristotelian conceptions of mimetic drama, but does so without recourse to such an array of specific literary predecessors.

In saying the above I am implicitly making a claim about Vvedensky's play, one that not all readers will accept. I am asserting that this "absurdist" play can and should be interpreted in a coherent manner. What is more, I am claiming that the analysis of subtextual references by the author can lead us toward a recognition of authorial intent, realizing of course that any such recognition is necessarily provisional and partial. Still, I do believe that Vvedensky had something relatively specific that he wanted to say in his play, something that was directly related to the unquestionably absurd world of the Soviet Union at the height of the purges. I think that he is able to express what he wishes to say about contemporary society through the images he provides of murdered children, whose deaths, which are treated in almost comic-book fashion in the play, take on meaning through their association with a literary and cultural tradition that gives childhood a particular valence in Russia. That is, I will take seriously Vvedensky's use of "children" in the play, and connect their situation with the historical and cultural uses of childhood in Russia.

To make his points, Vvedensky brings into contact two specific literary and cultural traditions, neither of which has been sufficiently appreciated by those who have written on this play. The first, evoked by the very title, is the Christmas story (*sviatochnyi rasskaz*), a popular genre in nineteenth-century Russian literature practiced both by specialists and by such classic Russian authors as Leskov, Dostoevsky, Chekhov, and even Nabokov. It was, of course, well known in European literature as well, with Charles Dickens's *A Christmas Carol* being perhaps the most famous example. Leskov provided a succinct description of the genre: "The Christmas Story must meet the following criteria: it must be connected to the Christmas period—from Christmas until Epiphany. It has to be in some way fantastic, has to have some kind of moral, at the very least to go against some dangerous superstition and, finally, it should end gaily."[6]

At first glance it would seem, then, that Vvedensky's play is a straightforward parody of the genre, for after making an obvious reference to the form Vvedensky provides a work that seems to lack any moral, and does not end gaily—to say the least. Nevertheless, in her analysis of Leskov's statement, Dushechkina points out that neither Leskov nor many other writers of Christmas stories necessarily followed all of the rules laid out here. In particular, she notes that many Christmas stories, both folkloric and traditional, "are filled with all kinds of deaths: the heroes die after telling fortunes that predict their death, wolves tear them to pieces, they freeze in the forest, drown in reservoirs or die of a heart attack after seeing corpses come to life."[7] One particularly important example of such a story, and perhaps the most famous Russian work in the genre, is Dostoevsky's "Malchik u Khrista na elke" (The Boy at Christ's Christmas Party), which was published in the January 1876 issue of *Diary of a Writer*. In this version a child, lost and freezing to death in St. Petersburg, has a vision of all the abandoned children of the city joining Christ himself for a Christmas party. The story, apparently one of Dostoevsky's personal favorites, combines in a particularly grotesque way the saccharine vision of the boy with the horrifying reality of his death. As such, although it is not quoted directly by Vvedensky, it may be considered a precursor to *The Ivanovs' Christmas Party*, which also manages to combine the good cheer of a traditional Christmas story with death.[8] Still, Dostoevsky's story does seem meant to provide a moral, at least to its readers, who are presumably expected to be shamed by the child's uncomplaining death into paying more attention to the plight of Russia's poorest and most vulnerable citizens. In the case of *The Ivanovs' Christmas Party* the moral is harder to find, although, as we will see, it is perhaps not impossible.

Dostoevsky's story, dealing as it does with a child and Christmas, is the crucial link with the other set of subtexts on which Vvedensky's play draws; that is, plays and stories in the Russian tradition in which children do not simply die but are murdered. A number of these works happen to be in the Russian dramatic canon, the most famous being Tolstoy's greatest drama, *Vlast' t'my* (*The Realm of Darkness*, 1886). The play tells the sad tale of Nikita Chilikin, a peasant workman who has an affair with his master's wife Aksinia. His evil mother Matrena thinks that her son will be able to move up in the world through this affair and she induces Aksinia to poison her already ill husband and marry Nikita. After the marriage, however, Nikita has an affair with Aksinia's daughter Akulina, and when this results in the birth of a child, Nikita, egged on by his evil mother, crushes the boy to death. Although the murder is not discovered and Akulina is to be married off to wash away her sin, Nikita cannot stand the burden of his guilt and he confesses his deeds before the entire community.

The initial stimulus for Tolstoy's play is generally regarded to have been the author's acquaintance with a trial that took place in 1880. Although it is well known that courts and trials were extremely important stimuli for Dostoevsky, it is less frequently recognized that a number of Tolstoy's later works, including the novel *Resurrection*, the novella "The Kreutzer Sonata," and the play *The Living Corpse*, are also creative reworkings of criminal proceedings.[9] In the instance of *The Realm of Darkness*, the connection to the actual events of the trial of Efrem Koloskov and Martha Ionova appears to be quite close. As Tolstoy put it in an 1896 interview:

> The subject of *The Realm of Darkness* was almost exactly taken by me from an actual criminal case that took place in the Tula court. I was informed of the details by my good friend Davydov, who was then the prosecutor and is now the judge of that court. . . . Just as it was presented in *The Realm of Darkness*, the case dealt precisely with the murder of a child who had been born to a stepdaughter, and, what is more, the murderer confessed publicly in just the same way at the marriage of his stepdaughter."[10]

As it happens, Davydov was not Tolstoy's only source of knowledge of the case. The author himself went to the Tula jail and interviewed the convicted murderer Koloskov sometime in 1881.

Nevertheless, as is usually true in such cases, the actual facts of a murder case were but one of the subtexts underlying Tolstoy's work. Indeed, the pattern of illicit sex, murder of a helpless victim (usually a child), and public confession that seems to link the actions of Koloskov and Tolstoy's Nikita is a paradigm that had been employed by Russian literature well before 1881. Tolstoy's reworking of the Koloskov trial is simultaneously a revisitation and reinterpretation of a pattern that had first surfaced in Russian dramatic literature in a play by Aleksei Pisemsky entitled *Gov'kaia sudbina* (A Bitter Fate, 1859). That work begins with the arrival in his home village of a peasant named Ananii who has been working in the big city for a number of years. He discovers that in the meantime his wife Lizaveta has been having an affair with his and her owner, the landlord Cheglov-Sokovin. As opposed to most stories of such liaisons, that of Lizaveta and Cheglov-Sokovin is not one of exploitation but of mutual love. Lizaveta was forced to marry her husband against her will and she and her owner now have a true relationship. Her husband, however, cannot accept the situation, and, after fruitless negotiations with the weak landowner, he returns to his hut where he seizes and murders the child that had been born to Lizaveta and Cheglov-Sokovin. After the murder he escapes, but he eventually returns to the village to confess—"You can run away and hide from human judgment but you can't escape God's."[11] In addition to containing the sex, murder, confession paradigm, this drama also features extensive use of peasant dialect. This was something completely unheard of in Russian drama at the time, and it would be used even more extensively by Tolstoy in *The Realm of Darkness*.

As one might expect, Tolstoy was aware of Pisemsky's drama. When it first came out, he said, "I liked Pisemsky's drama very, very much: wonderful, wonderful, strong and true to life, not invented."[12] Interestingly enough, when he reread the work in 1890, he came to a rather different conclusion, as a diary entry attests: "Read Pisemsky's drama *A Bitter Fate*. Bad."[13] A comparison of the two plays makes the reasons for Tolstoy's changed opinion of Pisemsky's work clear. One interesting fact about Tolstoy's reading practice is that he often read for potentials, seeing in works only what he wanted to see. When he read Pisemsky's drama in 1859, he must have seen in it the linguistic wealth and the power of the murder and confession scenes. What is more, he probably would have recognized the potential strength of the conflict within Ananii's mind, before, during, and after the murder, something that Pisemsky does not bring out in his drama. In rewriting Pisemsky's drama (keeping in mind his knowledge of the court case), Tolstoy completely dropped characters from the gentry sphere, narrowing the focus to the peasants. He banished the love element represented by Lizaveta and the landowner, and, in addition, he eliminated a farcical investigation scene that almost ruins Pisemsky's fifth act. Instead, he focused on the gradual psychological disintegration of Nikita, and created strong evil women characters (Matriona, Akulina, and Anisia) alongside him. Finally, in the characters of Akim and Mitrich, he created a certain counterweight to the play's blackness. After having accomplished all these revisions, Tolstoy was, presumably, incapable of recognizing anything of value in Pisemsky's play, for in his own mind he had now realized its potentials while avoiding its failures.

Nor were *The Realm of Darkness* and *A Bitter Fate* the only literary works that might have provided Vvedensky with ideas about how to craft his play. It is likely that his reading of Dostoevsky's *Crime and Punishment* played a part as well. As I noted above, one aspect of the dramatic situation that clearly interests Vvedensky, although true to OBERIU dramatic practice he did not delve into the psychological motivations, is the disintegration of the mind of the murderer, her sanity or insanity. This aspect, of course, is central to Dostoevsky's great novel. And while the story of Raskolnikov lacks the illicit sex segment of the paradigm that links Tolstoy's play to Pisemsky's and ultimately to Vvedensky's (actually, illicit sex is present in the novel in the aborted "incestuous" relationship between Raskolnikov's double Svidrigailov and his sister Dunia as well as in the trade we never actually see Sonia Marmeladova practice), it contains an abundance of material relating to the mind of the murderer as well as a scene of public confession. As in the case of Pisemsky's play, however, Dostoevsky's novel is not as unremittingly dark as Tolstoy's or Vvedensky's plays, balancing as it does the murder with the sentimentality of Marmeladov and the love story of Raskolnikov and Sonia.[14]

What is more, Tolstoy's play was not the final classic Russian literary work to employ the paradigm I have been discussing. In 1900, Anton Chekhov published a longish story entitled "In the Ravine" (*Vovrage*) that covers the same ground. Here we see the collapse of the Tsybukin family of merchants. The eldest son is a forger who is eventually arrested and sent to prison. He was married to Lipa with whom he had a child. The second son is a simpleton whose wife, Aksinia, cheats on him with various neighbors (i.e., illicit sex). In a fit of rage, she murders Lipa's child by throwing a tub full of boiling water on him (the scene is one of the most brutal in Russian literature). Chekhov breaks the paradigm, however, and darkens the story even further by eliminating the expected confession scene. Instead, Aksinia eventually pushes her father-in-law out of his house and appears to live happily ever after.

The general plot cluster I have been describing was featured at least one more time in the Soviet era in Evgenii Zamiatin's 1929 story "The Flood." Here we see a childless couple who become foster parents to a teenage girl. The male protagonist begins a sexual relationship with the foster child. His wife, Sofia, puts up with this until, after a flood on the Neva, she kills the foster child with the almost inevitable axe, chops up the body, and throws it in the river. Although she had previously been unable to conceive a child, she becomes pregnant almost immediately after the murder and eventually bears a girl. However, again following the paradigm initially laid out by Pisemsky, she is overcome with feelings of guilt and confesses publicly to her crime at the end of the story. Significantly, although Zamiatin's narrator does not provide any other motivation for the crime at the time of its occurrence than jealousy, when Sofia confesses she hints that another motivation was the nebulous belief that the death of her rival would somehow lead to her becoming pregnant (as indeed it did). Thus, she says, "I struck her with an axe. She was living with us, she was living with him, I killed her and I wanted to have . . ."[15] That is, the crime is committed, at least in part, because of a desire to have a child.

There can be no doubt but that Vvedensky had these works in mind when he wrote his play. As I noted above, Milivoe Iovanovich discovered a series of connections between the play and *Crime and Punishment*. They relate to the murder weapon in the first scene (an axe) and, in her view, the nanny's public confession in scene 5. The axe, of course, provides a link to *Crime and Punishment* as well as to Zamiatin's story, but the fact that the person murdered is identified as a child links Vvedensky's work to Tolstoy's or Pisemsky's play, rather than Dostoevsky's novel (although of course the murdered retarded sister of the pawnbroker does possess child-like traits). Furthermore, although public confession plays a role in all the works, the nanny's obvious peasant connections (through her putative fiancé, the woodcutter Fedor) again emphasize the connections with the dramatic tradition. What also connects Vvedensky's play to the works of Tolstoy, Pisemsky, and Chekhov is the effect produced by the deaths and their aftermath, despite the fact that in this regard Vvedensky's play seems at first quite different from the antecedent texts.

All of the literary works mentioned above count on the death or murder of a child to evoke horror in readers or spectators. This horror, in Russian audiences, is particularly deep because of a distinctive concept of childhood and children in Russian culture, a tradition that also had its beginnings in the work of Tolstoy. Thus, while the suffering or, at the greatest extreme, the murder of a child is found horrific in most cultures, in the Russian nineteenth-century context it is particularly shattering.[16]

And ultimately it is to changing views of the sanctity of human life, as figured here in the life of children, that Vvedensky is referring in his play.

As I have written about extensively elsewhere, from the mid-nineteenth century Russians had developed a specific attitude toward childhood and children.[17] Childhood in Russia was a literary invention, and it appeared more or less fully formed in the pseudo-autobiographical novel *Childhood* (1853) by Leo Tolstoy. In Tolstoy's view, which was amplified by a complementary one provided by Sergei Aksakov in 1856 entitled The *Childhood Years of Bagrov's Grandson*, childhood is supposed to have been the happiest stage of life, a time that can never be equaled by adult experience. Chapter 15 of Tolstoy's debut work begins with one of the most influential sentences Tolstoy ever wrote for the Russian cultural mind: "Happy, happy unforgettable time of childhood! How can one not love, not cherish its memories?" For the next eighty years, practically every first-person description of childhood in Russia, whether in fictional or nonfictional form, was oriented to them. Nineteenth-century autobiographers not only repeated Tolstoy's overall interpretation of childhood, they also borrowed typically Tolstoyan situations, cadences, and turns of phrase. Of course, to say that Tolstoy invented a paradigm that was used for understanding childhood by generations of Russians is not to imply that he invented this view out of whole cloth. Rather, it is likely that Tolstoy's vision had such staying power because it coincided with existing Russian views. In any case, it has become quite impossible to separate literary reality from real life, particularly because in a highly bookish country like Russia no one who sits down to recall his or her childhood, or who thinks about the kind of childhood society should provide does so without having Tolstoy's work in mind.

As a result of this paradigm, allowing a child to suffer was considered the worst of sins, a sentiment expressed most famously in Russia in this period by Dostoevsky, particularly in *The Brothers Karamazov*, where the fact of children's suffering is taken by Ivan to show God's absence or at least powerlessness. Of course, at the same time in *Brothers Karamazov* it is the death of the child Iliusha that allows for the fellowship of the other children under the aegis of Alesha Karamazov, so a suffering child can be redemptive as well. We can see the same paradigm at work in the plays of Pisemsky and Tolstoy. Although the confessions at the end of the play cannot bring the child back to life, they do indicate that some redemption can grow from the innocent suffering of the child, so the horror of the murder is in some sense softened. Chekhov, by contrast, at least implicitly, is polemicizing with his predecessors by failing to include a scene of redemption. The suffering of the child is irredeemably evil in "In the Ravine."

In the early Soviet period, however, the Tolstoyan tradition, understood to be a specifically gentry paradigm, was for a time eclipsed by the vision of childhood provided by Maksim Gorky in his pseudoautobiographical novel polemically entitled *Childhood*. Here the overall impression is one of childhood as a time of difficulty and hard knocks. In the Tolstoyan tradition, recalling childhood leads to nostalgically pleasant reminiscences. By contrast, for Gorky the past must be remembered in order for it to be "exposed to its roots and torn out of grim and shameful life—torn out of the very soul and memory of man."[18] Autobiography is not a nostalgic attempt at eternal return but a means of overcoming the past. Humankind, for whom the child is a synecdoche, is seen growing ever upward toward the sun, which provides the light for the "bright future." Gorky's work thus does not merely express the experience of a writer from a different socioeconomic background; it challenges the Russian notion of childhood as such.

A number of works written in the early Soviet period continued to undermine the traditional view of children and childhood as sacred. Perhaps the most famous of them is Fedor Gladkov's proto-socialist realist novel *Cement* (first published in 1925). In this work Gleb Chumalov comes back from the Civil War expecting to return to the life he had led before going off to fight. Instead, he discovers that in his absence his wife Dasha has become an active Communist party worker and that she has no desire to return to the patriarchal conditions of pre-revolutionary Russia. The central symbol of Russia's break with tradition is not, however, Dasha's liberation but rather her placement of their daughter Nurka in the Children's Home "Krupskaia." When Gleb first visits the home he is horrified to see what conditions are like:

From the verandah Gleb saw more children down below among the bushes and the clumps of ill-clad trees of early spring. The children were straying about like goats at the factory, fighting with each other, crying. Some groups were turning over the soil, digging greedily and hurriedly like thieves, glancing fearfully behind them. They would dig and dig and then turn and tear the booty from each other's grasp

The one who was stronger and cleverer would roll clear of the heap of little bodies and run aside with his loot, gnawing greedily, chewing and choking, tearing at it with his hands as well as his mouth." [19]

In the face of Gleb's dismay that Dasha could have allowed their child to live in such conditions, the liberated Dasha responds with a principled refusal to think of her child any differently than anyone else's: "In what way is Nurka any better than the others? She has had her hard times too." [20] In principle, Dasha wants all the children to have a good life, and she chastises the Children's Home workers for not providing one. In practice, however, although she sees that life in the home is killing her daughter, she refuses to take her back, putting her devotion to the Party and a new life for all above her personal concerns.[21] In the end, although Nurka does indeed die, the factory resumes cement production. Presumably, the novel's reader is meant to recognize that the personal sacrifice of Gleb and Dasha, while profound, counts for little in the grand scheme of things. After all, there are other children and they will inherit the glorious future.

The suffering child in *Cement* was in fact merely one particularly striking instance of a more general fact of Soviet life: individual human life was simply considered unimportant in the face of the inevitable flow of history. As Mark Steinberg put it in discussing the work of Andrei Platonov: "Platonov expanded the inspiring effects of suffering to embrace the whole of human experience: 'Despair, torment, and death—these are the true reasons for heroic human action and the most powerful motors of history. We must feel torment, millions must die, must fall from inexhaustible love, in order to obtain in ourselves the capacity to work." [22] In this environment it must have been exceptionally difficult for any author who wished to assert the importance of the individual to do so. While in the nineteenth century a play that described the death of a single child, as Pisemsky's or Tolstoy's had, could be expected to evoke horror, so much so that the horror had to be redeemed by a confession at the end, it is hard to imagine that readers in the 1930s could have been touched.

The question of children and their role in Soviet society was treated not only in fiction. Indeed, my guess, and this is only a guess, is that the immediate stimulus for writing a play in which "children" are treated as objects to be killed rather than cherished was not the series of plays and stories discussed previously that form the background subtexts of Vvedensky's work. Rather, what may well have brought the grotesque nature of Soviet reality into focus for him was a different play, one that was never actually staged at the time it was written, but that made quite a stir in Soviet theatrical circles nonetheless: Sergei Tretiakov's *Khochu rebenka* (*I Want a Baby*).[23] As summarized by Robert Leach:

> It tells the story of Milda, a Latvian Party worker, who wishes to contribute to the revolution by bearing a child, but has no wish for a husband . . . Milda chooses a good proletarian building worker, Yakov, to be the father of the child, though he is hardly a morally irreproachable Communist, and he has a fiancée as well. However, once he gets her with child, he becomes sentimentally paternal, until Milda dispatches him back to his girlfriend Lipa with a hit over the head. The last scene is set three years into the future, as Milda dreams of what may be. At the "Exhibition of Children," she receives the first prize, but it is shared with Lipa, and the next prize is won by the child of a drug addict, whom Milda had urged to have an abortion. As all the children are raised aloft, Yakov cries, in an uncanny premonition of Stalin (who was to become "Uncle Joe," provider of "happy childhoods"), "Hurrah for the heroes of our age!"[24]

According the Tretiakov, "the play isolates and examines dispassionately the expenditure of sexual energy which has as its aim the birth of a baby. It is not about how to give birth to the biggest baby possible, it is about how to give birth to the healthiest; it is about the direction of Soviet power."[25] That is to say, a baby is seen precisely as a symbol of the future. This is not, of course, a very original idea, but it is important to recognize that this play, written in 1926–27, already indicates a change in the Soviet conception of childhood, a change dictated by the very existence of the Soviet state, and one that doomed Gorky's version of childhood to the dust heap of history. This was for the simple reason that once the Soviet Union had been founded it was ideologically impossible to imagine an unhappy childhood. After all, if, as Stalin claimed, socialism had been "achieved and won" in the Soviet Union, then children must be being brought up in practically ideal conditions. Ergo, the kind of suffering the Gorkian pseudo-autobiographical alter ego had endured in the bad old prerevolutionary days could not serve as a model for children born in the Soviet Union after the consolidation of Soviet power. These children, the healthy sons and daughters of the Soviet state who are being displayed and measured at the end of Tretiakov's play, had to have a happy childhood by definition. And so, the traditional Russian myth of childhood as a happy time was fated to make a comeback, not precisely in Tolstoyan terms of course but in a formula that every Soviet child of the '30s and '40s was expected to know by heart: "Thank you for our happy childhood, Comrade Stalin."[26]

To a writer like Vvedensky, who had already been arrested twice by the time he wrote the play, the state's official concern with the happiness of children, manifest in the Stalin-era motto, must have seemed grotesque. It is therefore my claim that this play—connected not with the happiness but with the inexplicable suffering and death of children—is an evocation of grotesque Soviet reality, a description that is presented through the mediation of the Russian tradition of writing about suffering children. Children, the hope for the future in the Christian tradition, and the Russian literary tradition (for the most part anyway), and, according to official Soviet ideology of the 1930s, can do nothing but die in Vvedensky's work. And the fact that these children range in age from infancy to 82 indicates that in the grotesque world of the play, any and all humans can be in the helpless position of children, as indeed all of Soviet society was under the watchful eye of Stalin, the all-seeing patriarch.

The play eschews any attempt to evoke overt horror at the murders precisely because, in the context of the time, murder had become so commonplace. As the Doctor who examines the nanny's mental state and pronounces her perfectly sane despite her protestations to the contrary says: "Take her away and it would be better to bring in the Christmas tree. Swear to God it would be better. Gayer, somehow. Being on call is so boring. Good night" (p. 165). That is to say, the only possible way that Vvedensky could provoke in his potential audience the kind of reaction that Pisemsky, Tolstoy, and Chekhov were able to elicit in the nineteenth century was to multiply the murders of children in a completely unredeemed world, hoping against hope that precisely the absence of any emotional reaction inside the play could produce one outside of it.[27]

NOTES

1. OBERIU is an acronym for *Ob"edinenie real'nogo iskusstva* (Association for Real Art), which was a loosely organized Leningrad-based group that functioned between 1927 and 1930. Its most celebrated members (denominated collectively as OBERIUTY), in addition to Vvedensky, were Daniil Kharms and Nikolai Zabolotsky. Perhaps the best-known dramatic work to come out of this group was Kharms's play *Elizaveta Bam*.
2. Vvedensky, 1:157. Further references to this play will be made in the main text by reference to page numbers of this edition.
3. Iovanovich, p. 77.
4. Ibid, pp. 71–86.
5. Roberts, p. 105.
6. Quoted in Dushechkina, p. 95. Dushechkina has done by far the most comprehensive work on this genre in Russian literature. Interested readers should consult her *Russkii sviatochnyi rasskaz: stanovleniie zhanra.* (St. Petersburg: Sanktpeterburgskogo universiteta, 1995) and her collection of primary texts *Chudo rozhdestvenskoi nochi: Sviatochny rasskazy* (St. Petersburg: Khudozhestvennaia literatura, 1993) (coedited with Henryk Baran).
7. Dushechkina, pp. 98–99. This is true not only of Russian Christmas stories. Think, for example, of such well-known stories as Hans Christian Anderson's "The Little Match Girl," and "The Steadfast Tin Soldier," both of which end with a death.
8. Iovanovich notes a connection. Comparing the play with the last line of Dostoevsky's story, in which the narrator takes credit for imagining the scene presented, she says: "In sum, Vvedensky's parody is the refusal of the writer to imagine, or rather the depiction of the absurd-hellish world as the only possible and real sphere of activity" (p. 79).
9. See chapter 1 of this volume for a consideration of this issue in *The Living Corpse*.
10. Quoted in N. K. Gudzy's notes to *The Realm of Darkness* in Tolstoy, 26:706.
11. Pisemsky, 1959, 9:229. The play remained a staple of the Russian theatrical repertoire until well into the twentieth century.
12. Letter to Druzhinin of 20 December 1859; Tolstoy, 60:217.
13. Tolstoy, 51:98.
14. On the subject of Russian stories that use part or all of this paradigm, it is worth mentioning that Leskov's "Lady Macbeth of the Mtsensk District," discussed extensively in the previous chapter, employs it as well.
15. Zamiatin, "Navodnenie," 2:139.
16. At least in regard to suffering, it should be noted that while Americans in the twenty-first century might well agree, such feelings were by no means universal in nineteenth-century culture. Certainly in Britain and America, for example, it was felt that a bit of suffering was good for children, as the proverbial phrase "spare the rod and spoil the child" indicates.
17. A. Wachtel, 1991.
18. Gorky, p. 302
19. Gladkov, *Cement*, pp. 34–35.

20. Gladkov clearly believed in the Gorky vision of childhood as a necessary time of suffering as can be seen from his own pseudoautobiographical "Story about Childhood" published in the 1940s. There, practically quoting the master, he says at one point "And now, flipping through the book of my life, I am disturbed and I ask myself, is it necessary to tell about these long-past days, is it necessary to depict the cursed tortures in which I passed in my childhood and then my youth: . . . But the inner voice of conscience and duty assures me constantly: you must tell, must show the torturous thickets through which the people of my generation had to pass . . . in order to escape from the hellish darkness onto today's open road." Fedor Gladkov, "Povest o detstve" (Moscow, 1980), p. 215.

21. In his book, *Sex in Public: The Incarnation of Early Soviet Ideology*, Eric Naiman provides some interesting material on Soviet readers' reactions to Dasha's choice. Apparently, there was a great deal of disagreement on the matter, with some readers seeing her as a paradigm and others as someone to be castigated (see pp. 89–90).

22. Steinberg, p. 139.

23. Although Meyerhold and Terentiev both wanted to perform the play soon after it was written in 1926–27, neither ever managed to stage it, though El Lissitsky provided designs for a proposed Meyerhold production during the 1927–28 season. Nor was the play published, with the exception of two scenes that appeared in *Novyi LEF* in 1927. The full text of the play did not appear in Russian until 1988 in the journal *Sovremennaia dramaturgiia* no. 2, pp. 209–237.

24. Leach, p. 175.

25. Quoted in Leach, p. 177.

26. For discussions of changing attitudes toward childhood and children in the 1930s see Jeffrey Brooks, *Thank You, Comrade Stalin! Soviet Public Culture from Revolution to Cold War.* (Princeton, NJ: Princeton University Press, 2000), and Lisa A. Kirschenbaum, *Small Comrades: Revolutionizing Childhood in Soviet Russia*, 1917–1932 (New York: Routledge Falmer, 2001).

27. In this, Vvedensky can be seen as in sympathy with the efforts of his fellow OBERIU writer Daniil Kharms, whose technique in the stories of the 1930s has been described by Neil Carrick in terms of negative theology. See "Daniil Kharms and a Theology of the Absurd." (PhD dissertation, Northwestern University, 1993.)

CHAPTER 7

Banality Transformed: "Life with an Idiot"
on the Page and on the Stage

AS IS FREQUENTLY THE CASE WITH OPERAS, the story of Alfred Schnittke's *Life with an Idiot* does not begin with the time of its composition in the early 1990s. Rather, an investigation of this intriguing work must start with a discussion of the text on which the opera's libretto is based, the short story "Zhizn's idiotom" (Life with an Idiot), by the Russian writer Viktor Erofeev. But neither is the story the earliest place to begin, for, as we will see, the subtextual web woven by the story and its operatic transposition will take us back to numerous other points of origin in (mostly) Russian nineteenth- and twentieth-century culture.

Erofeev's story was written, according to the author, in 1980.[1] This was a particularly tense time in the late years of the Brezhnevian "age of stagnation," especially for Erofeev, since in 1979 he had been among the leading contributors to an independent almanac of Russian literature and visual art entitled *Metropol*. The contributors, including such luminaries as Vasilii Aksenov and Ernst Neizvestnyi, attempted to have the volume published officially in the Soviet Union, but when publication was denied, the volume appeared in the United States in both Russian and English. In the wake of the ensuing scandal, Aksenev was forced to emigrate and many of the other contributors found themselves in uncomfortable positions.[2] Erofeev himself was kicked out of the Soviet Writers' Union as a result of this affair. Given the perquisites that membership in this organization provided, this was potentially a difficult material blow, but it could well be argued that the notoriety Erofeev derived from the scandal was in the long run more valuable than his punishment was disabling.[3] In any case, the experience must have led him to recognize that any chances of a liberalization in Soviet cultural policy were remote and emboldened him over the next few years to produce work that was clearly well outside the bounds of what the Soviet censorship could find acceptable.

Erofeev was born 1947, the son of a high-placed Soviet diplomat. Thanks to his father's postings, he spent a good part of his childhood years in the West. As a result, he was exposed early on to much that was unknown to the vast majority of even educated Soviet writers. Although trained originally as a literary critic and specializing in such topics as the Marquis de Sade, Dostoevsky, and existentialism (the influence of all three would become glaringly obvious in his later literary work), Erofeev's real desire was to be a literary writer. While the phenomenon of literary-critic-turned-writer is also known in other countries (particularly since the spectacular success of Milorad Pavić and Umberto Eco), the model was especially tempting in Russia. On the one hand, this had to do with the exceptional prestige that literature and its producers had in Soviet society, as well as the spectacular success in this dual profession of Andrei Siniavsky/Abram Tertz. In the best of such cases, the literary critic is able to convey his understanding of how great literary works are fashioned into the creation of successful texts of his own. But such cases are rare and it is more usually the case that the critic's creation seems like an artificial bricolage composed of elements that do not fuse into a convincing whole.

Erofeev, in my view, belongs precisely to the group of critic/writers whose literary work is unconvincing, although there is no question that not everyone would agree with this opinion. Regardless of what one thinks of Erofeev's oeuvre as a whole, however, if we concentrate on "Life with an Idiot" I believe that it will be possible to demonstrate how much the story was improved in the process of becoming an opera libretto. But before we can discuss what is added by the operatic medium, we must first examine the original story as written by Erofeev. The story itself is relatively uncomplicated. Narrated in the first person, it begins by relating the narrator's "punishment" for an unclear crime; that punishment, regarded by the narrator and his friends as extraordinarily light, is that he must take into his family an "idiot" chosen by himself. He goes to a lunatic asylum and selects "Vova," whom he brings home to his recently acquired second wife. The main part of the story is devoted to describing how Vova destroys their life.

What strikes any reader immediately is the obvious political subtext of the story. The narrator, a member of the Russian intelligentsia, is being punished by an unnamed "them" (the government). While the permeability of the categories nomenklatura/intelligentsia was a fact of late Soviet life, one of the important myths of the intelligentsia (dating from the middle of the nineteenth century) was that these two worlds were utterly opposed. The intelligentsia, with writers as their avant-garde, saw themselves as forming a kind of "second government" (in the words of a character in

Solzhenitsyn's celebrated semidissident novel *The First Circle*). As a result, they were always liable to being "punished" by the first government.

At the same time, as the narrator later comes to realize, he is simultaneously being punished by his own desires (representative of the desires of the Russian intelligentsia as a whole), his pretence to do something important, something in keeping with the intelligentsia's self-perceived historical role. So, like the heroes of nineteenth-century novels who choose to rescue prostitutes to demonstrate their commitment to social reorganization, rather than choosing some harmless but boring idiot, the narrator looks for a mission and selects someone to save. Vova, the idiot he chooses, whose goatee, balding head, and diminutive body clearly identify him as a stand-in for Lenin, is himself a metonym for the Soviet state; later, in Ilya Kabakov's designs for the original operatic production, the connection with Lenin would be made transparent.[4]

In the best traditions of the nineteenth-century classics, the "intelligent" attempts to raise his idiot to a higher level of civilization—but in the course of the story he is instead swallowed up by the idiot, just as the intelligentsia who embraced the Bolshevik state were eventually destroyed by it. First, the idiot destroys his apartment (ripping up his library being the first step, of course). Then the idiot takes the man's wife, raping her in his presence (but she ultimately enjoys it, perhaps a sign that the thoroughly modern Erofeev is still after all a traditional Russian misogynist). Then he throws over the wife in favor of the intelligent himself. The two begin a homosexual relationship which culminates in the idiot's decapitation of the wife, the disappearance of the idiot, and the narrator's own apparent descent into idiocy.

This last section, of course, sounds like a rip-off of the finale of Fedor Dostoevsky's *The Idiot* (a novel whose importance to the story as a whole is signaled by the title). And this is by no means the only way in which Erofeev uses/abuses the Russian literary tradition. The narrative is filled with allusions to such texts as Gogol's "Diary of a Madman," Dostoevsky's "Muzhik Marei," Tolstoy's *War and Peace*, Turgenev's *Hunter's Notes*, and more. Indeed, at one point the narrator places the entire blame (or credit) for his situation on the Russian literary tradition. Discussing his preference for an idiot who would be more of a iurodovyi than a simple maniac, the narrator says, "Well, perhaps my ideal was not completely my own—there was, of course, some borrowing here: In the distance I could see glimmers of a church in Zagorsk, and after all from the days of our childhood we've all been lapping up the same literary milk."[5]

In his story, Erofeev tries to balance these quotations and allusions to the Russian high cultural tradition and his heavy-handed allegory with liberal doses of gratuitous sex, violence, and obscenity. These last three are, by the way, Erofeev's usual stock in trade, and appear to be designed to shock the supposedly staid Soviet and post-Soviet reader. In the end, however, this story simply does not hang together convincingly. The allegory is too obvious, the quotations are too heavy-handed, the self-flagellation is disingenuous, and in general the story simply takes itself far too seriously.

So how did this mediocre story come to be an opera libretto and what happens to it in the process of transposition? According to his own testimony, Schnittke heard Erofeev read the story and immediately saw its potential as material for an opera. He requested Erofeev to rework the story as a libretto. While it is unclear exactly how much influence the composer had on the revisions, we can see that the transposition allowed potentials inherent but unrealized in the original (particularly its historical and cultural depth) to come to the surface; it also makes them artistically convincing by the addition of real irony and self-irony, the grotesque and the humorous.[6] To an extent, this happens as the result of changes on the purely textual level, but even more so it happens because of the very nature of operatic transposition.

Schnittke, as his statements reveal, was aware of what was going on, even simply on the textual level:

> Viktor Erofeev wrote the libretto. It differs pretty substantially from his story. Specifically—a wonderful touch—he introduces a new character: Marcel Proust. Being a talented person, Erofeev immediately sensed everything necessary for an opera. Specifically, repetition, as in a doubling or tripling repetition of words and situations. Because in an opera anything that flits by only once fails to be recognized. It needs to be emphasized by means of repetition. And that repetition can either be serious or farcical. Here I would say it leans toward the farcical. But the text is paradoxical—and thus a farcical drama with farcical repetitions can turn out to be even more tragic than a normal drama."[7]

This last formulation, by the way, is extremely close to one that was used by Iakov Tugenkhold in his revue of the premiere of the ballet *Petrushka* in 1911: "The performers were so imbued with the seriousness of this 'puppet' drama that they were able not only to *amuse* the spectator through the strangeness of their 'cardboard' rhythms but to force him to sympathize with the romantic *tragedy* of Petrushka-Pierrot."[8] That is, in both cases the addition of comic and even farcical elements allows the inherent tragedy to come through more clearly.

We will return to Stravinsky and ballet a bit later when we discuss some specifically musical aspects of the opera, but one other connection with the Ballets Russes productions should be mentioned here: for the opera's first production Schnittke was able to bring together an all-star cast of which Diaghilev himself would have been proud. It consisted of the conductor Mstislav Rostropovich, stage director Boris Pokrovsky, and stage designer Ilya Kabakov.[9] Kabakov's presence in particular appears to have had an important effect on the opera, lending it a certain conceptualist irony that had been lacking in the original story.

Before returning to Stravinsky, let us take a deeper look at the types of things Schnittke noted in his statement about Erofeev's reworking of the story text, repetitions for example. In the story, just after the passage quoted earlier in which he acknowledged that he borrowed his vision of the proper type of idiot, one whose pathology would be "*narodnaia po forme i soderzhaniiu*" (national in form and content), from the Russian literary tradition, the narrator adds in a rather bathetic vein: "*Strashno zhit' na belom svete, gospoda*" (life in the wide world is horrifying, gentlemen). This is a clear allusion to Nikolai Gogol's story "How Ivan Ivanovich Quarreled with Ivan Nikiforovich," which ends "*skuchno na etom svete, gospoda*" (this world is boring, gentlemen). As is often the case with Erofeev, however, although the subtextual allusion is obvious, its relevance to the action at hand is not clear. That is to say, knowledge of Gogol's story does not deepen our appreciation for Erofeev's. Rather the quote is, if anything, a red herring.

In the operatic version, a large percentage of the narrator's speech is cut. This, in addition to conforming to normal operatic practice (operatic librettos are generally more compact than their source texts) has the immediate positive effect of deemphasizing the annoying garrulousness of the original. In particular, the narrator's overt recognition of his relationship to the Russian literary tradition is eliminated. It is replaced by the more subtle device of repeating, and thereby emphasizing, the obvious quoted lines, which are usually given to the "Chorus of Friends." These friends are mentioned in the beginning of the story version, but as the whole thing is narrated by the first-person voice of the unnamed intelligent, they do not play much of a role. In the opera, as an embodied, on-stage presence, they seem to be a grotesque combination of Greek chorus and Monty Python farce, commenting on the action through mock serious repetitions of the narrator's sentences. Overall, their repetition of the narrator's literary quotes makes the borrowed textual material seem completely bathetic and therefore deflates it.

If we carefully examine the section of the opera in which this Gogol quotation appears, this effect will become clearer. First, we note the fact that the "*strashno zhit'*" quote has been brought closer to the Gogol by the elimination of the adjective "*belyi*" (the addition of which, by the way, was totally unmotivated in the story). Furthermore, the quote, whose use out of context in Erofeev's story recalled the Belinskian idea of Gogol as social critic—never mind that Belinsky used a different quotation from "The Overcoat" taken out of context to make his point—can no longer be taken seriously. This is because of its "farcical" repetition by the Chorus of Friends (emphasized by the music), whose presence to utter this thought cannot be motivated by any realist interpretation of the opera. At the same time, the grotesque and ultimately funny combination of realism and farce is underscored by Schnittke's musical text, for the music that accompanies the words "*narodnaia po forme i soderzhaniiu*" is strikingly Mussorgskian in stark contrast to what could be called the "post–Lady Macbeth of Mtsensk" coloration of the score as a whole.[10]

From this early section of the opera, let us move to the brilliant stage trick of the appearance of Proust. In the story, Proust appears symbolically as the favorite reading of both the narrator's wives. "Proust" is then a metonymic stand-in for such conceptions as modernist belief in the autonomy of art and with the salvific potentials of memory, all of which is shattered by the idiot. The destruction of the narrator's library and in particular the novels of Proust begins the cascading course of events that will end in the rape of the wife, the narrator's homosexual affair with the idiot, the murder of the wife, and the narrator's own descent into idiocy.

In the opera this whole scene (which is marked "Tempo di Tango") is given a comic touch through the onstage appearance of Marcel Proust. Most hilarious, if we are thinking of the role of repetition, is the repeated exchange between the narrator's wife and Proust. She begins, "Oh, my God, he ripped up all of Proust," which elicits Proust's line "Oh, my God, he ripped me up."[11] Overall, this realized metonym seems to be derived more from Monty Python than from the operatic tradition, and it clearly lends a strong comic undertone to the opera.

At the same time, however, it would be wrong to believe that the operatic version of Erofeev's story serves only as a comic deflation of a one-dimensional source text. This occurs, but simultaneously we can see that the musical version also deepens and makes Erofeev's story more serious by bringing out new levels of meaning. As an example, let us examine the music Schnittke provides for the opera's entr'acte. While in the story the murder of the wife happens once, in the opera it appears twice. Or, to put it more accurately, the narration of act 1 brings us to the point of her being killed before breaking off (her actual murder will occur in act 2). At the climactic moment just before the end of act 1, however, when the murder has been thoroughly prepared and should by rights take place, Schnittke interrupts the action with his entr'acte.

From one perspective, this is merely a transparent device to build dramatic tension and as such is not remarkable. From another, the choice of music for this section is surprising and highly marked. The entr'acte (which, by the way, appears on the recording of the opera but is not to be found in the published score for reasons I have not been able to ascertain) is a tango with a prominent solo violin part. To be sure, audiences could have a variety of associations with tango music, but my own immediate reaction was to link Schnittke's music with the "Tango" section of Stravinsky's ballet/fairy tale "L'Histoire du Soldat." Stravinsky's is, of course, a story of temptation, a Faust story, and this association helps us to recognize that Erofeev's text is itself a variation on the Faust theme (though no reference to Goethe's *Faust* can be found in the text). After all, the narrator's problems result from his having given in to the temptation of the state (Mephistopheles) to accept a complex idiot whom he can potentially save and from whom he can potentially learn (and from whom he does learn, in a sense), rather than having chosen just a simple idiot. What is more, the idea of the Mephistophelian bargain of intellectuals with the state is a subtext of *The Master and Margarita*, a novel that is itself also filled with operatic subtexts.

Following this line of thought we might not be surprised to discover that in order to compose "Life with an Idiot" Schnittke interrupted work on a Faust opera he had been writing for years and would eventually premiere only in 1995. The extent to which these two projects were connected in Schnittke's mind, however, can perhaps be seen in the following excerpt of a conversation recorded by Aleksandr Ivashkin. Schnittke says: "*Faust* is really an enigma for me, like *Peer Gynt* [a version of which he was also working on in parallel to "Life with an Idiot"], and like another of my ideas—the ballet *John the Baptist*, on the subject of Salome. I once had a plan (now almost abandoned) to write a one-act ballet for the Salzburg Festival as a companion piece to *The Soldier's Tale* (*L'Histoire du soldat*)."[12]

With this quotation in mind we can reconstruct some of the associative chain that attracted Schnittke to Erofeev's story. This will help us to understand, first of all, why Schnittke was captivated by such a mediocre text in the first place, and, simultaneously, how the opera managed to bring out so many latent potentials in that text. Salome, of course, is linked to Erofeev's story through the image of the severed head. The erotic potential of this object is particularly central to Strauss's operatic version, which ends with the famous "Dance of the Seven Veils." For Schnittke, then, Erofeev's story could be linked to an earlier text (and one that had been successfully transposed into opera) that follows the line linking the severed head with eroticism. Furthermore, that text was clearly connected in Schnittke's mind with Stravinsky's *L'Histoire*, as his versions of both were to be on the same (unrealized) program. And both of these were linked to *Faust* as a group of enigmatic texts on which the composer either was working or wished to work (the connections with *Peer Gynt* are less clear to me).

The appearance of the Stravinsky-like tango in the opera, then, signals that for Schnittke at least Erofeev's story actualized all of these potential intertexts. I would insist, however, that none of them is actually present in the original story, a fairly banal text whose subtexts are purely one-dimensional (almost all drawn from nineteenth-century classic Russian literature). That is, we have here a fortuitous case in which Erofeev's story more or less accidentally resonated with a series of texts that obsessed Schnittke. Primarily through his musical device of introducing the Stravinskian tango, the composer deepened Erofeev's story, connecting it to a major West European tradition.

Thus, the operatic transposition of Erofeev's story leads in two directions simultaneously. One of them injects a levity that was absent in the original, producing a farce that in Schnittke's words is "more tragic than a normal drama." The other leads in the direction of deepening and making more serious and varied the subtextual world of Erofeev's story, an effect accomplished primarily on the musical rather than on the textual level. The result is an opera that—while perhaps not fully successful—has achieved a stage life beyond that of its composer, and one that deserves careful consideration for its successful navigation of the difficulties of textual transposition.

NOTES

1. The story appears in a number of places including the collection *Russkaia krasavitsa. Roman, raskazy* (Moscow: Molodaia gvardiia, 1994), pp. 292–313. References to the story will be made in the main text of this chapter by reference to page numbers in this edition. The translations are mine.
2. For a contemporary description of the events, see Gerd Ruge, "The Case of the 'Metropol' Writers," *Encounter* (January 1980): pp. 74–77.
3. Erofeev provided his own version of the events in a story entitled "A Murder in Moscow: A Cold War Family Story," *The New Yorker* (27 December 1999, pp. 48–57).
4. Kabakov's designs for the costumes of the central characters were reproduced in the program book published by De Nederlandse Opera Stichting in 1992.
5. Erofeev, p. 293.
6. In Schnittke's view, "'Life with an Idiot' is not a closed, but rather an open text." (as quoted in *Alfred Schnittke zum 60. Geburtstag – Eine Festschrift* [Hamburg: Internationale Musikverlage Hans Sikorski, 1994], p. 79). This openness, in my view, is primarily a function of Schnittke's rereading rather than an inherent feature of Erofeev's text.
7. Ivashkin, 1994, p. 186.
8. Quoted in A. Wachtel, 1998, p. 40.
9. This production was preserved in a 2-CD recording by Sony (S2K 52495).
10. In the sound recording, this section can be found on disc one [NB: in at least some sets, the discs are mislabeled so 1 is 2 and vice versa], about 2 minutes into the fourth track. In the score this section can be found on pages 19–22 (See Alfred Schnittke, *Das Leben mit dem Idioten. Oper in 2 Akten* [Hamburg: Musikverlag Sikorski, 1992]).
11. Disc 2, from about 1 minute to 1:40 into track 4. In the score, p. 86.
12. Ivashkin, *A Schnittke Reader*, p. 34.

CONCLUSION:
Intertextual Expectation

EXPECTATION IS AN INTEGRAL PART of the reading experience. As we begin to read a text we immediately, almost without thinking, begin to classify it and to compare it to others with which it appears to share a family resemblance. If we begin a large book in prose, for example, we expect it to be a novel. Depending on its title, its linguistic register, the way the story begins, we mentally assign it to a subgenre, and much of our reading pleasure has to do with our recognition of how and in what ways this novel conforms to or differs from our expectations of that genre. Authors of fiction can exploit these expectations in a variety of ways depending on their goals. Someone trying to write a best-selling thriller is well aware that certain rules involving, say, pace, size, and style cannot be seriously toyed with. The trick is to come up with new and exciting plot twists within the fairly narrow constraints of the genre. A reader familiar only with classic Victorian novels would have a difficult time appreciating what the author of our imagined thriller was up to, but those readers who had read many such novels would have no difficulty appreciating both what is innovative and what remains the same.

Poetry works in much the same fashion. For poets: "genre remains an invaluable tool for understanding both individual poems and the poetic tradition. A poet seeking to express his or her thoughts invariably retains or revises the paradigms of earlier poets. Likewise, readers encountering a new work will try to make sense of it by comparing it to things they already know."[1] In addition to expectations created by genre and meter, poets can and do create intertextual expectations through citations of small but recognizable pieces of previous poetic works. Russian poetry makes particularly intensive use of such intertextual links. As my colleague Ilya Kutik has put it, "Russian poets like to clap each other on the back, sometimes across many centuries. They do so either by citing each other, either on the level of the use of poetic epithets, or on the level of poetic 'topics.'"[2]

Drama, probably the least-studied literary form these days, functions as do prose and poetry. Theater audiences (as well as readers of plays) are encouraged in a variety of ways to guess as to what will unfold on the stage and on the page, and much of the pleasure of the theatrical experience revolves around this guessing game. The intertextual connections explored in this book uncover a particular subset of expectations that are created primarily by reference to thematic (rather than generic or linguistic) clusters. In the works considered here, authors tell stories that, for the most part, already existed in the cultural repertoire of the contemporary Russian audience. Through their inclusion of references to earlier versions of a given story, they invite readers or audiences to compare the new version with previous incarnations. The plural *incarnations* is quite important here, because the plays about which I speak do not merely place themselves in opposition to a single earlier work as a way of creating a parody or stylization of an individual predecessor. Rather, insofar as they refer to a number of predecessor texts that employed the same theme or story line, the audience or reader cannot be certain of the importance or role of any particular predecessor. Indeed, the meaning of the new work is created not so much from the story told as from the interaction of that story with previous versions.

Thus, each of the dramatic texts considered here acts as a nexus of intertextual play, a space in which various versions of a single general story line can interact to create a new synthesis—which itself can become a freestanding version of the story. In the case of *Petrushka*, for example, although most Russian audience members would have assumed a relationship between the ballet and the Russian folk puppet show from the title alone, the ballet quickly invokes a series of texts drawn from other traditions—twentieth-century rewrites of the traditional *commedia dell'arte* and famous nineteenth-century chestnuts of the ballet and operatic repertoire. The audience is invited to see the new work as an unexpected synthesis that borrows directly from some traditional versions of the story line while polemicizing with others. The meaning of the ballet, as I have tried to show, cannot be understood merely by reference to what happens on the stage. The ballet makes much more sense if we understand the ways in which its authors assumed that the audience would compare what was taking place before them with other potential versions of the story that are alluded to through the stage action. In particular, they were meant to see how the ballet was positioned between high and low cultural versions of the Petrushka story. We find something similar going on in the operatic version of "Life with an Idiot," which works precisely because the subtextual expectations evoked by the libretto simultaneously inject a degree of low-cultural buffoonery and high-culture seriousness into what was originally a fairly banal story.

In their book *Mikhail Bakhtin: Creation of a Prosaics*, Gary Saul Morson and Caryl Emerson build on Bakhtin's insights to set out a comprehensive theory of "double-voiced discourse."[3] In relation to literary work, their central point is that when an author uses a word (and this can easily be expanded to a trope, a theme, a genre, and so forth), he or she cannot do so "innocently"; the word is always colored by some or all of its previous uses. For Bakhtin, of course, the novel was the central genre, and he was particularly fascinated by the use of double-voiced discourse in Dostoevsky's novels. This preference for the novel led him to discount the potential of other forms to exploit double-voiced discourse in order to create expectation and meaning. What I have demonstrated here, I believe, is that Russian modernist drama made particularly intensive use of double-voicing, generally but not always on the level of narrative units or clusters, in order to drive audience expectations and create dramatic meaning. Even a writer creating as absurd a play as Vvedensky's seems to have counted on the fact that his audience would understand the action of his drama against the backdrop of other Russian works that dealt with childhood on the one hand and on the other with Christmas stories. In dialogue with this background, *The Ivanovs' Christmas Party* makes a certain kind of sense; absent such a dialogue, it is indeed theater of the absurd.

It is impossible, when discussing works of this kind, to avoid the question of authorial intent. In my view, and as should have been abundantly clear in my analyses, authors insert the intertextual linkages we find in these plays intentionally. They choose to create dramatic works that exploit existing literary stories (and sometimes extraliterary sources) to direct audience expectations. To some extent, these stories were "in the cultural air," and thus could conceivably have been drawn upon by accident, un- or semiconsciously; however, the ways in which they are juxtaposed betray a conscious attempt to create meaning through their dialogue. Insofar as I insist on the conscious work of the author, my vision of the author differs substantially from that proposed by many poststructuralist European critics for whom "ends, aims, or intentionality were the *bête noir* . . . to be removed for good by the death of the author and the assurance that there was nothing outside the text."[4]

What is more, I am claiming that an understanding of how a given author uses subtextual references in a drama can lead us toward a coherent interpretation of a particular work. Unless one sees how the web of subtexts employed in a drama leads to an overall interpretation, the only point of recognizing them is as part of an academic parlor game of the "can you top this" variety. Nevertheless, the fact that authors know what they are doing does not necessarily mean that they know why they are doing it. Nor can they necessarily be sure of the cultural capacity of their contemporary or future audiences, or those audiences' attitudes to the various source texts. Thus there can be little doubt that Shostakovich not only recognized that his version of the Lady Macbeth story was related to Shakespeare's version (and Leskov's rewrite of it) but also to the modernist versions of Zamiatin and Kustodiev. However, to say that he knew this does not mean that he knew in any conscious way that his attraction to Kustodiev's rethinking of the story was related to its eroticization. And there is no doubt at all that he was unaware, or unable to predict, that his Soviet audience would not be able to swallow that eroticization. Moreover he could not have guessed that his work would later come to symbolize the absurdity of Stalinist-era artistic repression and as a result enjoy a belated popularity when that repression finally disappeared.

Two final questions remain to be considered. Is the type of intertextual play I describe here particularly suited to dramatic work? And is there something about the Russian literary tradition that makes it especially partial to an intensive exploitation of intertextuality? My provisional answer to both questions is a qualified yes. It seems clear that the type of expectational play I describe could not occur in lyric poetry. In his voluminous work on intertextuality in Russian modernist poetry, Igor Smirnov has attempted to demonstrate that authors in a given period or school have a tendency to base their poems on an implied juxtaposition of predecessor texts from two different traditions. If this is true, then we can understand it as a variation of what I have described here. Yet, the differences are even more significant. In the dramas I describe, the locus of intertextual activity is the theme or story line, while lyric poets refer to their predecessors by citations of words or word clusters. What is more, at least in Smirnov's view, they do so according to regular patterns whereas dramatic authors seem far more opportunistic and flexible.

Drama differs from lyric poetry, then, in the level at which it employs intertextual reference, focusing more on thematic than linguistic connections. One might imagine that novels could and would do something similar; and indeed, as I noted earlier, Bakhtin insists that the novel is the only genre that can fully exploit the potentials of double voicing. It is not my intention to polemicize with Bakhtin and his interpreters, but it is my supposition that the length of the novel makes it difficult for it to employ multiple jux-taposed subtexts, at least at the thematic level described here. The standard dramatic work must be graspable by the audience (and potential reader) as a whole that lasts no more than two or three hours. The novel, meant to be read over days, weeks, or months, is not nearly as concentrated an art form, a circumstance that makes it difficult to sustain the kind of intensive intertextual dialogue we find here. Nevertheless, there are clearly some modernist novels that could be fruitfully analyzed in this context. Andrei Bely's *Petersburg* for example, which situates itself at the nexus of Petersburg narratives from Pushkin, to Gogol, to Dostoevsky, juxtaposing them with Petersburg mythology drawn from the 1905 Revolution as well as subtexts from the author's own life, seems to function quite similarly to the dramas described here. Thus, while it does appear that the use of inter-textual clusters to structure the reading or spectating experience is perhaps more frequent in drama, it can be found in other literary forms, including the novel and most likely also including narrative poems as well.

Finally, there is the question of the specificity of the Russian tradition. The strongly citational nature of the Russian poetic tradition has been noted by a number of scholars, and this study certainly points to the citational nature of Russian drama, at least in the twentieth century. Compared to most other European cultures, Russian literature has a short and focused history, with literary activity strongly concentrated in the two cultural capitals Moscow and St. Petersburg. The producers of Russian literature have tended to develop strong links with each other, links that often cross media boundaries. One could easily speculate that such a brief and intensive history encourages a literary culture particularly attuned to intertextual reference and a readership able to appreciate such references. The fact that much of intertextual theorizing was developed by scholars whose central interest was the Russian tradition provides powerful induc-tive evidence that there is something about the tradition that lends itself to such analysis. Nevertheless, one could clearly find examples of similar types of intertextual play at work in many other literary traditions, though perhaps at a lower level of intensity.

What then, does an appreciation of the intertextual substrate of the plays analyzed here reveal? First and foremost it tells us something about what the author of the play had in mind, although we are well aware that any such understanding is partial and provisional, not only because of our own limitations but also because the author him- or herself cannot control the text's meaning. Still, recognizing the double-voiced play of the text allows us to move toward a coherent interpretation of a work, albeit an author-centered one. Furthermore, given that the more culturally competent of contemporary audience members likely possessed a similar horizon of expectations, our recognition of the expectations that a given narrative cluster was likely to engender may help us to understand the original reception of a given play. To be sure, these plays can be enjoyed even by readers or audiences who are unfamiliar with the tradition inside of which the plays were written. However, the pleasure of the culturally competent reader, who recognizes the potential relationship between the story and an earlier version or versions, is augmented by the play of expectations engendered through the comparison.

This knowledge, however, is only a starting point, for there is inevitably a large gap between authorial intent (even assuming that the analysis approaches an understanding of it) and textual meaning. This was true even at the time and in the culture in which the play was created, and it grows larger with time and translation. It is the job of the interpreter, be he a reader of the text or a director who intends to stage the work, to rethink for a contemporary audience in a given time and place the implications of the intertextual play that these dramatic texts invite. After all, even if I have managed to elucidate what Tolstoy was trying to say in calling up the story of faked suicide, and even if many of his contemporaries might have appreciated this, a director staging Tolstoy's *Living Corpse* in New York in 2006 simply cannot count on her audience to respond to the hints that Tolstoy included in the text. On the other hand, she may be able to exploit fears of identity theft that are, for audiences in our day, far more salient than they were for Tolstoy's contemporaries. Thus, in the end the intertextual dialogue I describe here can be seen as an invitation for contemporary readers, directors, and actors. This invitation does not necessarily have to be accepted or acted upon, but there is no doubt that if it is appreciated the knowledge gained should change the way these and other Russian plays are read, savored, and staged.

NOTES

1. Michael Wachtel, p. 146.
2. Ilya Kutik: "Tri veka russkoi poezii: Kakoi zhe iz nikh 'zolotoi'?"
   http://max.mmlc.northwestern.edu/~mdenner/Demo/project.htm (translation mine).
3. Morson and Emerson, 1990, pp. 136–163.
4. Orr, p. 52.

Alekseev-Iakovlev, A. Ia. *Russkie narodnye guliania*. Leningrad: 1948.

Auslander, [. . .]. "Bal 'Satirikona'." *Apollon* No. 6, 1910, pp. 35–36.

Bachinskaia, Nina. *Narodnye pesni v tvorchestve russkikh kompositorov*. Moscow, 1962.

Barricelli, Jean-Pierre, ed. *Chekhov's Great Plays: A Critical Anthology*. New York: New York University Press, 1981.

Bartlett, Rosamund, *Wagner and Russia*. Cambridge, UK: Cambridge University Press, 1995.

Beaumont, Cyril W. *Michel Fokine and His Ballets*. London: C. W. Beaumont, 1935. Reprinted as *Michel Fokine and His Ballets*. New York: Dance Horizons, 1981.

———. *The Diaghilev Ballet in London*. London: Putnam, 1940.

Bely, Andrei. "*Formy iskusstva.*" *Simvolizm kak miroponimanie*. Moscow, 1994, pp. 90–105.

Bely, Andrei. *Vospominaniia o Bloke*. Moscow: Respublika, 1995.

Benois, Alexandre. *Reminiscences of the Russian Ballet*, trans. Mary Britnieva. London: Putnam, 1941.

———. *Memoirs*, trans. Moura Budberg. 2 vols. London: Chatto and Windus, 1964.

———. *Aleksandr Benua razmyshliaet*. Moscow, 1968.

———. *Moi vospominaniia*. 2 vols. Moscow, 1990.

Berkov, B. N. *Russkaia narodnaia drama*. Moscow, 1953.

Blok, Aleksandr. *Stikhotvoreniia*. Leningrad, 1955.

———. "The Unknown Woman." In Tim Langen and Justin Weir, trans. and ed., *Eight Twentieth-Century Russian Plays*, pp. 39–64. Evanston, IL: Northwestern University Press, 2000.

Boretz, Benjamin, and Edward T. Cone, eds. *Perspectives on Schoenberg and Stravinsky*. Princeton: Princeton University Press, 1968.

Børtnes, Jostein. "Male Homosocial Desire in *The Idiot*." In Peter Alberg Jensen and Ingunn Lunde, eds., *Severnyi sbornik*, pp. 103–120. Stockholm: Almquist & Wiksell International, 2000.

Bowers, Faubion. *Scriabin*. 2 vols. Palo Alto, CA: Kodansha International, 1969.

Bowlt, John E. *The Silver Age: Russian Art of the Early Twentieth Century and the "World of Art" Group*. Newtonville, MA: Oriental Research Partners, 1979.

Bowlt, John E., trans. and ed. *Russian Art of the Avant Garde*. New York: Thames and Hudson, 1988.

Brown, Edward J. *Mayakovsky: A Poet in the Revolution*. New York: Paragon House, 1988.

Brown, Malcolm H., ed. *Mussorgsky: In Memoriam 1881–1981*. Ann Arbor: UMI Research Press, 1982.

Buckle, Richard. *Diaghilev*. New York: Atheneum, 1979.

———. *Alexandre Benois 1870–1960: Drawings for the Ballet*. London: Hazlett, Gooden & Fox, 1980.

Bulgakov, Fedor Ilich. *Al'bom russkoi zhivopisi: kartiny K. E. Makovskogo*. St. Petersburg: A. Suvorin, 1892.

Bulgakov, M. *Master i Margarita*. Moscow, 1973.

Carlson, Maria. *"No Religion Higher than the Truth": A History of the Theosophical Movement in Russia*. Princeton, NJ: Princeton University Press, 1993.

Carlson, Marvin. "Invisible Presences: Performance Intertextuality." *Theatre Research International* 19 no. 2 (1994): pp. 111–117.

Chances, Ellen. "Chekhov's *Seagull*: Ethereal Creature or Stuffed Bird?" In *Chekhov's Art of Writing: A Collection of Critical Essays*, edited by Paul Debreczeny and Thomas Eekman. Columbus, OH: Slavica, 1977.

Chekhov, Anton. *Letters of Anton Chekhov*. Trans. by Michael Henry Heim with Simon Karlinsky. New York: Harper & Row, 1973.

Chekhov, A. P. *Polnoe sobranie sochinenii i pisem v tridtsati tomakh*. Moscow, 1974–1983.

Chernyshevsky, N. G. *Chto delat'?*. Leningrad, 1975.

Chudakova, M. O. *Zhizneopisanie Mikhaila Bulgakova*. Moscow, 1988.

Clayton, J. Douglas. *Pierrot in St. Petersburg*. Montreal: McGill University Press, 1994.

Compton, Susan P. *The World Backwards: Russian Futurist Books, 1912–16*. London: British Museum Publications, Ltd., 1978.

Davydov, N. V. "*Iz vospominanii o L.N. Tolstom*." Sbornik vospominanii o L. N. Tolstom. Moscow, 1911.

Debreczeny, Paul, and Thomas Eekman, eds. *Chekhov's Art of Writing: A Collection of Critical Essays*. Columbus, OH: Slavica, 1977.

Diachkov, L. S., ed. *I. F. Stravinsky: Stat'i i materialy*. Moscow, 1973.

Dobuzhinsky, M. V. *Vospominaniia*. New York: Put' Zhizni, St. Seraphim Foundation, 1976.

Dostoevsky, F. M. *Polnoe sobranie sochinenii v tridtsati tomakh*. 30 vols. Leningrad, 1972–1986.

Donchin, Georgette. *The Influence of French Symbolism on Russian Poetry*. The Hague: Mouton & Co., 1958.

Druskin, Mikhail. *Russkaia revoliutsionnaia pesnia*. Moscow, 1954.

Dushechkina, E. V. " 'Ot sviatochnogo rasskaza nepremenno trebuetsia' (N. S. Leskov i traditstiia russkogo sviatochnogo rasskaza)." *Russkaia literature i kul'tura novogo vremeni*. St. Petersburg: Nauka, 1994.

Ehre, Milton. *Oblomov and His Creator: The Life and Art of Ivan Goncharov*. Princeton, NJ: Princeton UP, 1973.

Ehre, Milton, trans. and ed. *Chekhov for the Stage*. Evanston, IL: Northwestern University Press, 1992.

Elpat'evsky, S. Ia. "Vospominaniia o L've Nikolaeviche Tolstom." In N. N. Gusev and V. S. Mishev, eds., *L. N. Tolstoi v vospominaniiakh sovremennikov*. 2 vols. Moscow, 1955; vol. 2, pp. 138–46.

Emerson, Caryl. *Boris Godunov: Transpositions of a Russian Theme*. Bloomington: Indiana University Press, 1986.

Erdman, Nikolai. *Samoubiitsa*. Ann Arbor, MI: Ardis, 1980.

Erofeev, Viktor. *Russkaia krasavitsa. Roman, raskazy*. Moscow: Molodaia gvardiia, 1994.

Etkind, M. G. *Aleksandr Nikolaevich Benua 1870–1960*. Leningrad-Moscow, 1965.

———. *A. N. Benua i russkaia khudozhestvennaia kul'tura kontsa XIX—nachala XX veka*. Leningrad, 1989.

Etkind, M. G., ed., *Boris Kustodiev*. Moscow: Sovetskii khudozhnik. 1982.

Evreinov, Nikolai. *Veselaia smert'*. St. Petersburg: no date, but before 1910.

Farkas, Ann. "The Russianness of 'Petrouchka.' " *Artforum* 16 (January 1978), pp. 42–48.

Fedorov, N. F. *Filosofiia obshchego dela*. 2 vols. London: Gregg International Publishers, 1970.

Fels, Florent. "Un entretien avec Igor Stravinsky à propos de l'enregistrement au phonographe de *Pétrouchka*." *Nouvelles litéraires* December 8, 1928.

Fokine, Michel. *Fokine: Memoirs of a Ballet Master*. Trans. by V. Fokine. Ed. A. Chujoy. Boston: Little, Brown, 1961.

———. *Protiv techeniia*. Leningrad, 1962.

Frank, Joseph. *Dostoevsky: The Years of Ordeal*, 1850–1859. Princeton, NJ: Princeton University Press, 1983.

Garafola, Lynn. *Diaghilev's Ballets Russes*. New York: Oxford University Press, 1989.

Gasparov, Boris, Robert Hughes, and Irina Paperno, eds. *Cultural Mythologies of Russian Modernism: From the Golden Age to the Silver Age*. Berkeley: University of California Press, 1992.

Gladkov, Fedor. *Cement*. Trans. by A. S. Arthur and C. Ashleigh. New York: Frederick Ungar Publishing, 1960.

Gogol, Nikolai V. *Sobranie sochinenii v semi tomakh*. Moscow, 1984.

Gorky, Maxim. *Childhood*. Trans. by Margaret Wettlin. London: Oxford University Press, 1961.

Green, Martin, trans. and ed. *The Russian Symbolist Theater*. Ann Arbor, MI: Ardis, 1986.

Green, Martin, and John Swan. *The Triumph of Pierrot*. New York: Macmillan, 1986.

Grigoriev, Serge Leonidovich. *The Diaghilev Ballet, 1909–1929*. London: Constable, 1953. Reprinted as *The Diaghilev Ballet, 1909–1929*. Harmondsworth: Penguin, 1960.

Grossman, Joan. *Valery Bryusov and the Riddle of Russian Decadence*. Berkeley: University of California Press, 1985.

Gusev, N. N. *Dva goda s L. N. Tolstym*. Moscow, 1912.

Gustafson, Richard. *Leo Tolstoy, Resident and Stranger: A Study in Fiction and Theology*. Princeton, NJ: Princeton University Press, 1986.

Hamilton, David. "Igor Stravinsky: A Discography of the Composer's Performances." *Perspectives of New Music*, vol. IX/2–X/1, 1971.

Hamm, Charles, ed. *Petrushka: An Authoritative Score of the Original Version: Backgrounds, Analysis, Essays, Views, Comments*. New York: Norton, 1967.

Iampolski, Mikhail. *The Memory of Tiresias: Intertextuality and Film*. Trans. by Harsha Ram. Berkeley: University of California Press, 1998.

Iarustovsky, B. M., ed. *I. F. Stravinskii: stat'i i materialy*. Moscow, 1973

Iastrebtsev, V.V. *Vospominaniia*. 2 vols. Leningrad, 1959–60.

Ivanov, Viacheslav. *Sobranie sochinenii.* 4 vols. Brussels, 1971–1987.

Iovanovich, Milivoe. "Vvedenskii-parodist: K razboru Elki u Ivanovykh." *Wiener Slawistischer Almanach* 12 (1983).

Ivashkin, A. V. *Besedy s Al'fredom Shnitke.* Moscow: RIK 'Kul'tura', 1994.

Ivashkin, Alexander, ed. *A Schnittke Reader.* Trans. by John Goodliffe. Bloomington: Indiana University Press, 2002.

Jackson, Robert Louis. "Chekhov's *Sea Gull*: The Empty Well, the Dry Lake, and the Cold Cave." In Jean-Pierre Barricelli, ed., *Chekhov's Great Plays: A Critical Anthology.* New York: New York University Press, 1981.

Janacek, Gerald. *The Look of Russian Literature.* Princeton, NJ: Princeton University Press, 1984.

Jensen, Peter Alberg, and Ingunn Lunde, eds., *Severnyi sbornik.* Stockholm: Almquist & Wiksell International, 2000.

Karlinsky, Simon. "A Hollow Shape: The Philosophical Tales of Prince Vladimir Odoevsky." *Studies in Romanticism* 5, no. 3 (1966).

———. *The Sexual Labyrinth of Nikolai Gogol.* Cambridge, MA: Harvard University Press, 1976.

———. "Stravinsky and the Russian Pre-Literate Theater." *19th-Century Music* VI, no. 6 (Spring 1983), 232–240.

Katsell, Jerome H. "Chekhov's *The Seagull* and Maupassant's *Sur l'eau.*" In Jean-Pierre Barricelli, ed., *Chekhov's Great Plays: A Critical Anthology,* pp. 18–34. New York: New York University Press, 1981.

Kelly, Catriona. "From Pulcinella to Petrushka: The History of the Russian Glove Puppet Theatre." *Oxford Slavonic Papers,* new series, vol. XXI, 1988, pp. 41–63.

———. *Petrushka: The Russian Carnival Puppet Theatre.* Cambridge, UK: Cambridge University Press, 1990.

Kelly, Catriona, and Stephen Lovell, eds. *Boundaries of the Spectacular: Russian Verbal, Visual, and Performance Texts in the Age of Modernism.* Cambridge, UK: Cambridge University Press, 1999.

Kennedy, Janet. *The "Mir iskusstva" Group and Russian Art 1898–1912.* New York: Garland Publishing, 1977.

Khardzhiev, N. "Poèziia i zhivopis'." In *K istorii russkogo avangarda.* Stockholm: Hylea Prints, 1976.

Knapp, Liza, ed. *Dostoevsky's "The Idiot": A Critical Companion.* Evanston, IL: Northwestern University Press, 1998.

Kochno, Boris. *Le Ballet en France du quinzième siècle à nos jours*. Paris: Hachette, 1954.

Kozitskaia, Ekaterina. *Smysloobrazuiushchaia funktsiia tsitaty v poeticheskom tekste*. Tver, 1998.

Krasovskaia, V. *Russkii baletnyi teatr nachala XX veka*. Leningrad, 1971.

Kushlina, O. B. *Russkaia literatura XX veka v zerkale parodii*. Moscow, 1993.

Kuznetsov, E. M. *Russkie narodnye gulianiia po rasskazam A. Ia. Alekseeva-Iakovleva*. Leningrad, Moscow, 1948.

Lachmann, Renate. *Memory and Literature: Intertextuality in Russian Modernism*. Trans. by Roy Sellars and Anthony Wall. Minneapolis: University of Minnesota Press, 1997.

Langen, Timothy, and Justin Weir, trans. and ed. *Eight Twentieth-Century Russian Plays*. Evanston, IL: Northwestern University Press, 2000.

Lakond, Wladimir, ed. *The Diaries of Tchaikovsky*. New York: Norton, 1945.

Lakshin, V. *Tolstoy i Chekhov*. Moscow, 1975.

Leach, Robert. *Revolutionary Theatre*. New York: Routledge, 1994.

Lee, Vernon. *Studies of the Eighteenth Century in Italy*. New York: Da Capo Press, 1978.

Leifert, A.V. *Balagany*. Petrograd, 1922.

Levinson, André. 1913. "O starom i novom balete." *Ezhegodnik imperatorskikh teatrov*. 1:1–20.

———. *Ballet Old and New*. Trans. by Susan Cook Summer. New York: Dance Horizons, 1982.

Lieven, Prince Peter. *The Birth of the Ballet Russes*. Trans. by L. Zarine. London: George Allen and Unwin, 1936.

Lukashevich, S. *N. F. Fedorov (1828–1903): A Study in Russian Eupsychian and Utopian Thought*. Newark, DE.: University of Delaware Press, 1977.

Mariamov, A. "Zhiznenyi sluchai i literaturnyi siuzhet." *Voprosy literatury* 6 (1970): pp. 89–122.

McLean, Hugh. *Nikolai Leskov: The Man and His Art*. Cambridge, MA: Harvard University Press, 1977.

McLean, Hugh, ed. *In the Shade of the Giant*. Berkeley: University of California Press, 1989.

Medvedev, Pavel. *Dramy i poemy Al. Bloka*. Leningrad, 1928.

Meierkhol'd, V. E. "O teatre." In *V. E. Meierkhol'd: Stat'i, pisma, rechi, besedy*. 2 vols. Moscow, 1968.

Meyerhold, E. E. *Meyerhold on Theatre*. Trans. and ed. with a critical commentary by Edward Braun. London: Methuen & Co. Ltd., 1969.

Morson, Gary Saul. *The Boundaries of Genre*. Evanston, IL.: Northwestern University Press, 1981.

———. "Prosaic Chekhov: Metadrama, the Intelligentsia, and *Uncle Vanya*." *TriQuarterly* 80 (Winter 1990–91): pp. 118–159.

———. *Narrative and Freedom: The Shadows of Time*. New Haven: Yale University Press, 1994.

Morson, Gary Saul, and Caryl Emerson. *Mikhail Bakhtin: Creation of a Prosaics*. Stanford, CA: Stanford University Press, 1990.

Müller, B. *Absurde Literatur in Russland: Entstehung und Entwicklung*. Koln, 1978.

Naiman, Eric. *Sex in Public: The Incarnation of Early Soviet Ideology*. Princeton, NJ: Princeton University Press, 1997.

Nekrylova, A. F. *Russkie narodnye gorodskie prazdniki, uveseleniia i zrelishcha*. Leningrad, 1988.

Nest'ev, Izrail. *Zvezdy russkoi èstrady*. 2nd ed. Moscow, 1974.

Nijinska, Bronislava. *Bronislava Nijinska – Early Memoirs*. Trans. and ed. by Irina Nijinska and Jean Rawlinson. Intro. by Anna Kisselgoff. New York: Holt, Rinehart & Winston, 1981.

Nijinsky, Romola. *Nijinsky*. London: Sphere Books, 1970.

Nikitin, V. "Bogoiskatel'stvo i bogoborchestvo Tolstogo." *Prometeia* 12 (1980): p. 123–130.

Odoevsky, V. F. *Muzykal'noe-literaturnoe nasledie*. Moscow, 1956.

Oinas, Felix J. "East European Vampires." In *Essays on Russian Folklore and Mythology*, pp. 111–120. Columbus, OH: Slavica Publishers, 1985.

Olearius, Adam. *The Voyages and Travels of the Ambassadors, rendered into English by John Davies of Kidwelly*. London, 1662.

Orr, Mary. *Intertextuality: Debates and Contexts*. Oxford, UK: Blackwell, Polity Press, 2003.

Paperno, Irina. *Chernyshevsky and the Age of Realism*. Stanford, CA: Stanford University Press, 1988.

Paperno, Irina, and Joan Delaney Grossman, eds. *Creating Life: The Aesthetic Utopia of Russian Modernism*. Stanford, CA: Stanford University Press, 1994.

Pisemsky, Aleksei. *Sobranie sochinenii v deviati tomakh*. Moscow, 1959.

Poe, Edgar Allan. *Complete Stories and Poems*. Garden City, NY: Doubleday & Company, 1966.

Poliakova, E. *Teatr L'va Tolstogo*. Moscow, 1978.

Porudominsky, V. *I. N. Kramskoi*. Moscow, 1974.

Prokofiev, S. S., and N. Ia. Miaskovsky. *Perepiska*. Ed. by M. G. Kozlova and N. R. Iatsenko. Moscow, 1977.

Pushkin, Aleksandr. *Polnoe sobranie sochinenii*. 17 vols. Leningrad, 1937–1959.

Pyman, Avril. *The Life of Aleksandr Blok*. 2 vols. New York: Oxford University Press, 1979–1980.

Reiss, Françoise. *Nijinsky ou la grace*. Paris: Librairie Plon, 1957.

Rimsky-Korsakov, Andrei. *N. A. Rimskii-Korsakov: Zhizn' i tvorchestvo*. 5 vols. Moscow, 1946.

Rimsky-Korsakov, Nikolai. *Sbornik russkikh narodnykh pesen'*. Paris: Bessel, n.d.

———. *My Musical Life*. Trans. by Judah A. Joffe. New York: Knopf, 1947.

Ritter, Naomi. *Art as Spectacle: Images of the Entertainer Since Romanticism*. Columbia, MO: University of Missouri Press, 1989.

Roberts, Graham. *The Last Soviet Avant-garde: OBERIU – Fact, Fiction, Metafiction*. Cambridge, UK: Cambridge University Press, 1997.

Rozik, Eli. "The Interpretative Function of the 'Seagull' Motif in *The Seagull*." *Assaph. Section C. Studies in the Theatre* 4 [1988], pp. 55–81.

Rudnitsky, Konstantin. *Russian and Soviet Theater 1905–1932*. New York: Harry N. Abrams, Inc., 1988.

Russkoe narodnoe iskusstvo v sobranii Gosudarstvennogo Russkogo muzeia. Leningrad: Khudozhnik RSFSR, 1984.

Sakharov, V. I. "Lev Tolstoi i V. F. Odoevskii." In *Tolstoi i literatura narodov Sovetskogo Soiuza*. Erevan, 1978.

Sbornik populiarneishikh russkikh narodnykh pesen'. Leipzig: Zimmermann, 1921.

Schahadat, Schamma. *Intertextualit und Epochenpoetik in den Dramen Aleksandr Bloks*. Peter Lang: Frankfurt am Main, 1995.

Scholl, Tim. *From Petipa to Balanchine: Classical Revival and the Modernization of Ballet*. London: Routledge, 1994.

The Serge Lifar Collection of Ballet Set and Costume Designs. Comp. by Mary C. Palmer and Samuel J. Wagstaff. Hartford, CT: Wadsworth Atheneum, 1965.

Shapiro, Anne Dhu, ed. *Music and Context: Essays for John M. Ward*. Cambridge, MA: Department of Music, Harvard University, 1985.

Shklovsky, V. B. "Konstantin Eduardovich Tsiolkovsky." *Zhili-byli*. Moscow, 1964.

Shlifshtein, S., ed. *Miaskovskii: Avtobiografiia, stat'i, zametki, otzyvy (Sobranie materialov v dvukh tomakh)*. 2 vols. 2nd ed. Moscow, 1964.

Shostakovich, D. D. *Sobranie sochinenii v sorok dvukh tomakh*. 42 vols. Moscow, 1980–1987.

Smirnov, Igor. *Porozhdenie interteksta*. Saint Petersburg, 1995.

Solov'ev, Vladimir. *Literaturnaia kritika*. Moscow, 1990.

Steinberg, Mark D. *Proletarian Imagination: Self, Modernity, and the Sacred in Russia, 1910–1925*. Ithaca, NY: Cornell University Press, 2002.

Sternin, G. Iu., ed. *Abramtsevo*. Leningrad, 1988.

Stone-Nakhimovsky, Alice. *Laughter in the Void: An Introduction to the Writings of Daniil Kharms and Alexander Vvedenskii*. Vienna: Wiener Slawistischer Alamanach, 1982.

Stravinsky, Igor. *An Autobiography*. New York: Simon & Schuster, 1936.

Stravinsky, Igor, and Robert Craft. *Expositions and Developments*. London: Faber & Faber, 1959.

———. *Memories and Commentaries*. London: Faber & Faber, 1959.

Stravinsky, Vera, and Robert Craft. *Stravinsky in Pictures and Documents*. New York: Simon & Schuster, 1978.

Sukhovo-Kobylin, A. V. "*Smert' Tarelkina*." In *Trilogiia*, pp. 210–283. Moscow, 1959.

Swan, Alfred. *Russian Music and Its Sources in Chant and Folk Song*. New York: Norton, 1973.

Taranovsky, Kiril. *Essays on Mandel'stam*. Cambridge, MA: Harvard University Press, 1976.

Taruskin, Richard. *Opera and Drama in Russia: As Preached and Practiced in the 1860s*. Ann Arbor, MI: UMI Research Press, 1981.

———. "*Chez Pétrouchka*: Harmony and Tonality *chez* Stravinsky." *19th-Century Music*, X:3 (Spring 1987).

———. "The Unmaking of Lady Macbeth." *San Francisco Opera Program*, 1988.

———. *Stravinsky and the Russian Traditions: A Biography of the Works Through Mavra*. Berkeley: University of California Press. 2 vols. 1996.

Teatr: Kniga o novom teatre. St. Petersburg, 1908.

Tolstoy, L. N. *Polnoe sobranie sochinenii*. 90 vols. Moscow: 1930–58.

Tolstoy, Leo. *What Is Art?* Trans. by Aylmer Maude. Indianapolis, IN: Bobbs-Merrill, 1960.

Tynianov, Iury. *Arkhaisty i novatory*. Ann Arbor, MI: Ardis, 1985.

Tugenkhol'd, Ia. "Itogi sezona," *Apollon* No. 6, 1911, pp. 65–74.

Vershina, Irina. *Rannie balety Stravinskogo*. Moscow, 1967.

Vlasova, R. I. *Russkoe teatral'no-dekoratsionnoe iskusstvo nachala XX veka*. Leningrad, 1984.

Volkov, N. *Meyerhold*. 2 vols. Moscow, 1929.

Volkov, Solomon. *Testimony: The Memoirs of Dmitri Shostakovich*. Trans. by Antonina W. Bouis. New York: Harper & Row, 1979.

Vulfius, P. A., ed. *Russkaia mysl' o muzykal'nom fol'klore*. Moscow, 1979.

Vvedensky, Aleksandr. *Polnoe sobranie sochinenii*. 2 vols. Ann Arbor, MI: Ardis, 1980.

Wachtel, Andrew. "Death and Resurrection in *Anna Karenina*." In Hugh McLean, ed., *In the Shade of the Giant*, pp. 100–114. Berkeley: University of California Press, 1989.

———. *The Battle for Childhood: Creation of a Russian Myth*. Stanford, CA: Stanford University Press, 1991.

———. "Meaningful Voids: Facelessness in Platonov and Malevich." In Catriona Kelly and Stephen Lovell, eds., *Boundaries of the Spectacular: Russian Verbal, Visual, and Performance Texts in the Age of Modernism*, pp. 250–277. Cambridge, UK: Cambridge University Press, 1999.

———, ed. *Petrushka: Sources and Contexts*. Evanston, IL: Northwestern University Press, 1998.

Wachtel, Michael. *The Cambridge Introduction to Russian Poetry*. Cambridge, UK: Cambridge University Press, 2004.

Wanner, Adrian. *Baudelaire in Russia*. Gainesville: University Press of Florida, 1996.

Warner, Elizabeth. *The Russian Folk Theater*. The Hague: Mouton, 1977.

Westphalen, Timothy C. *Lyric Incarnate: The Dramas of Aleksandr Blok*.

London: Harwood, 1998.

Wigzell, Faith. "Folk Stylization in Leskov's *Ledi Makbet Mtsenskogo uezda.*" *The Slavonic and East European Review* 67(2): pp. 169–181, 1989.

Winner, Thomas G. "Chekhov's *Seagull* and Shakespeare's *Hamlet*: A Study of a Dramatic Device." *American Slavic and East European Review* 15 (February 1956): pp. 103–111.

Wright, A. Colin. *Mikhail Bulgakov: Life and Interpretations.* Toronto, ON: University of Toronto Press, 1978.

Youens, Susan. "Excavating an Allegory: The Texts of *Pierrot Lunaire.*" *Journal of the Arnold Schoenberg Institute*, Vol. VIII, No. 2, November 1984, pp. 95–116.

Zamiatin, Evgenii. *Sochineniia.* 2 vols. Munich: A. Neimanis, 1982.

Zatsarny, Iury, ed. *Russkie narodnye pesni: pesennik.* vol. VII, Moscow, 1987.

Zguta, Russell. *Russian Minstrels: A History of the Skomorokhi.* Philadelphia: University of Pennsylvania Press, 1978.